Conflict Resolution

Teaching Children to Work Together

By Caroline Lenzo
Kristin Oakes
Jackie Carpas
Melissa Hughes

Carson-Dellosa Publishing Company, Inc.
Greensboro, North Carolina

Credits

 **Editor**
Sabena Maiden

 **Layout Design**
Jon Nawrocik

 **Cover Design**
Matthew VanZomeren

 **Artists**
Bill Neville
Erik Huffine
Ray Lambert
Betsy Peninger
Julie Kinlaw

 **Cover and Inside Photos**
© Corbis Images
Photo www.comstock.com
© 1999 EyeWire, Inc. All rights reserved

ISBN 0-88724-870-5

Table of Contents

Caring Community: Creating an Inviting Atmosphere

Constructive Communication: Talking About the Tough Stuff

Positive Personals: Encouraging Good Behavior

Imperfect Incidents: Dealing with Difficult Situations

Introduction

Schools and communities are becoming increasingly diverse. Differences in family structures, ethnic backgrounds, and individual experiences can present a broad range of conflicts among students at school. Children need to be taught as early as possible how important it is to respect one another and value human differences. Building positive social skills is an integral part of child development. As students enter school and begin to interact with a larger circle of peers, friendships provide a strong foundation for their developing attitudes toward cooperating with others and solving conflict.

Positive peer interaction can also have a significant impact on a child's attitude towards school. The academic benefits of successful relationships with teachers, parents, and other children are demonstrated very early in education. Children who learn how to maintain satisfying friendships seem to enjoy school, participate more freely in a variety of different activities, and learn how to manage competition and conflict.

Conflict Resolution: Teaching Children to Work Together is packed with daily strategies and activities that teachers can implement in their classrooms to foster healthy friendships and promote appreciation for individuality. The topics include friendship, communication, expectations, emotions, atmosphere, behavior, and conflict. Because teachers often don't have the time to incorporate lengthy units into the curriculum, simple activities are provided that teachers can use to establish the kind of learning environment in which students will be most successful throughout the year. Bulletin board display ideas, reproducibles, literature suggestions, and ideas for parental involvement are also included to make this a helpful tool for every elementary teacher.

By fostering healthy social and emotional development, teachers can help children recognize and promote valuable citizenship skills. This resource is invaluable to teachers and caregivers who are interested in helping children make and keep friends, addressing their conflicts productively, showing them how to make independent choices, and teaching children to work together.

Friendship Fun: Setting Class Tone

Getting to Know Each Other

First Day Test

On the first day of school, students are often nervous about meeting their new teacher and classmates. Announce to the class that you will be giving a fun test and that they will all make a 100! Have students take out a piece of paper and pencil. Ask them questions about yourself and the school, such as: What is my favorite food? Where is our cafeteria? What is our school's mascot? After the "test," discuss the answers as a way to introduce both yourself and school procedures. Tell students that they each get a 100 for their great guesses! Students enjoy learning about their new teacher, and this activity is a great ice breaker!

Name Mobiles

Students can introduce themselves and learn each other's names with name mobiles. Show them how to make overlapping balloon letters. Explain to the class how to draw block letters that spell out names, and then cut the letters out along the outside edge, only leaving the overlapped portions connected (see below left). Give students a large piece of poster board to print their names and demonstrate for them how to cut out the group of letters. Next, tell students to draw pictures of things that begin with the letters in their names. Have them cut out the pictures. You can also provide students with magazines, greeting cards, and old illustrated calendars to cut out pictures to paste on each letter. Hole punch the top of the pictures and string yarn through the holes so the pictures can hang from the appropriate letter in each student's name. Depending on the ability level of students, the pictures can start with each letter of their names or indicate a particular interest of that child. Hang the mobiles from the ceiling in the room. These mobiles not only provide great name reminders for new classmates, but this also makes a great display for Open House or Parent's Night.

Memory Box

Read *Wilford Gordon McDonald Partridge* by Mem Fox (Kane/Miller Book Publishers, 1991) to your class. This story is about a little boy who helps an older woman remember by placing objects in a box that help trigger special memories. Discuss the special items that were placed in the box and why they were important.

Have each student prepare a memory box of her own. The outside of the box can be decorated to reflect the student. Make sure the student's name is clearly written on the outside of the box. The boxes can be made in class using shoe boxes, empty coffee cans, or paper lunch bags. When students bring in their special items, they can share with the class why each item was selected for their memory box. Items might include photographs, stuffed animals, small gifts, cards, or objects found outdoors, such as an acorn or a seashell, that remind them of places or events.

Materials for decorating:

contact paper	glitter pens
glue	magazines
wrapping paper	buttons
markers	construction paper
wallpaper scraps	crayons
stickers	material scraps

All About Me Bingo

Bingo provides a great way for students to learn about each other. Give students each a bingo sheet that identifies their hobbies, pets, etc. (see page 8). Then, provide time for students to find someone else in class who has written the same response in a square. When this happens, the students write their initials on each other's matching square. Students continue finding out about each other as they try to get "bingo" in a row, then return to their seats. Finish the game by discussing what things classmates have in common and what things make certain students unique.

All About Me Bingo

Fill up the bingo squares below. Then, find classmates that have the same answers, and have them initial the appropriate squares. When you have BINGO in a row across, down, or diagonally, return to your seat so we can share!

favorite color	favorite food	favorite game	the month of your birthday
your eye color	number of pets	car rider or bus rider?	the state you were born in
favorite movie	middle initial	favorite toy	favorite book
best subject	favorite TV show	favorite animal	favorite hobby

There are often times in the day when there are just a few minutes to fill with a quick, educational lesson. Here are some ideas that with the help of a few materials, can promote a kind community in minutes! Decide if it would work better as a large group activity with a lot of teacher direction or to have materials available in a small group setting. If you opt for small groups, the other students, when not working with the teacher, can read silently, work at other stations or centers around the classroom, or complete assignments with a buddy or independently.

Paper Plate People

Help students get to know each other and learn the positive things that others think about them. Provide each student with a plain paper plate. Have students draw their faces in pencil on the front of the paper plates. When complete, pass around each plate to classmates who should write positive characteristics on the back of the plate that describe the person. Remind students that they should use appropriate, positive comments. Brainstorm examples with the group. (Before returning the plates to the owners, read the comments.) After the plates are returned, students can further decorate them with crayons, markers, yarn, and construction paper. Glue a craft stick to the back of the bottom of each plate so that the plate can be used as a mask.

Other ways to use the paper plate masks:

- Make a book with the paper plate face used as the cover of the book and additional plates as book pages.
- Select one student's mask each week to display on a special student recognition bulletin board.
- Have classmates make positive comments on videotape to send home with each student to share with family.
- Students can write friendly letters to the students who made the most kind comments on their masks.
- Make a border from the masks to frame various bulletin boards throughout the year.
- Have parents make masks at Parent's Night and display them next to their children's masks.

Bag Buddies

Help students get to know the qualities "inside" their friends and not just what their classmates are like on the outside. Give each student a brown paper lunch bag and an index card. Using yarn, cloth scraps, construction paper, and markers, have students decorate the outsides of the bags to look like themselves. Then, have them write descriptions of their personalities, likes and dislikes, interests and hobbies, and favorite things on their index cards and place the cards inside their bags. Finished bags can sit on each child's desktop or be placed in a designated place in the classroom, where students can open up each bag to find out about each other's special characteristics that are tucked away on the inside.

Personal Pizza Pies

Show children that we each have characteristics that make us unique. This activity provides a nice visual for students to see this. Remind students how a pizza is made of several separate slices that make up a whole. Then, explain that each person is like a special pizza, made up of his own special characteristic "slices." Allow students to create mini pizzas that describe themselves. Provide paper plates, scissors, construction paper, glue, markers, and crayons. Instruct students to divide the plate into six to eight pizza slices using a black marker and a ruler. Inside each slice, students can write an interesting characteristic or other information about themselves. Using paper pizza topping shapes, students can write words or symbols that relate to each characteristic. Encourage them to emphasize their personalities and interests over their physical attributes. Display the Personal Pizzas around a bulletin board and talk about how the "slices" are similar and different. As a class, make a large class pizza, showing the unique qualities that make up the class. Each student's name can be listed on a large paper topping to represent each student. Display the class pizza on the bulletin board to show the variety and unity in the class.

Name Poetry

Name poems are another way for students to share information about themselves. Begin by modeling the process using your own name on a first draft. Write the letters of your name vertically on the board. Use each letter of your name to start each line of your poem. You may want younger students to write descriptive words, while older students can write phrases or sentences. After you have written a complete draft of your name poem, write a final draft. Write your poem so that the letters in your name stand out. Then, students can make their own name poems. Consider having students complete this activity on a computer. This would provide the perfect time to point out certain font, point size, and graphics features of word processing programs that students will use during the year. If you have a scanner or digital camera, students could place a photo of themselves on the page. After students have completed their poems, display them around the room or compile them into a class book. Students will enjoy seeing their work as well as learn new information about their classmates!

J olly
O rganized
E nergetic
Y our friend

Interest Inventories

Interest inventories are great, quick tools to find out information about your students. After you decide what you want to discover about your young learners, you can tailor an inventory to meet your needs. For example, if you would like to develop a reading program based on student preferences, create a reading interest inventory. If you are curious about students' study skills, adapt an inventory to assess work habits. The possibilities are endless. Of course, kindergarten students who are just beginning to print will require a much simpler inventory than an accomplished third grader. Modify the directions and inventories of the samples provided to fit your students. If creating lifelong learners is a goal you have for students, it is easier to achieve if you take the time to affirm and encourage student interests! Be sure to read, respond, and use information gathered on these inventories. Students learn quickly that you care about them when you show a genuine interest in them. Ideas can also be shared with parents at conferences and used to form groups for class projects. See sample inventories on pages 12-16.

Name_____   Date_____

The Bear Facts

1. What is the best movie you have ever seen?

2. What is your favorite book?

3. What do you like to do after school?

4. How often do you watch TV?

5. What is your favorite food?

6. Do you collect anything? If so, what?

7. What do you like to do in school?

8. What kinds of games/sports do you play?

9. Do you like to read for fun?

10. What else would you like for me to know about you?

Bee Yourself
Reading Inventory

Directions: Complete the following sentences.

My favorite book is _____ .

I love it because _____ .

Two other books I really like are _____

_____ .

Directions: Circle all answers that apply to you.

I really like to read . . .

biographies	fables	poetry
mysteries	fairy tales	animal stories
sports books	myths	books about history
science fiction	adventures	riddle and joke books
magazines	newspapers	

Directions: Underline the word that describes you.

1. I like to read.	often	sometimes	never
2. I like to read nonfiction.	often	sometimes	never
3. I like to read picture books.	often	sometimes	never
4. I like to read chapter books.	often	sometimes	never
5. I like to hear picture books.	often	sometimes	never
6. I like to hear chapter books.	often	sometimes	never
7. I like to reread my favorites.	often	sometimes	never

Fun Faces

Directions: Beside each statement, color the face that describes how you feel about each activity. On the back of this paper draw your favorite thing about school.

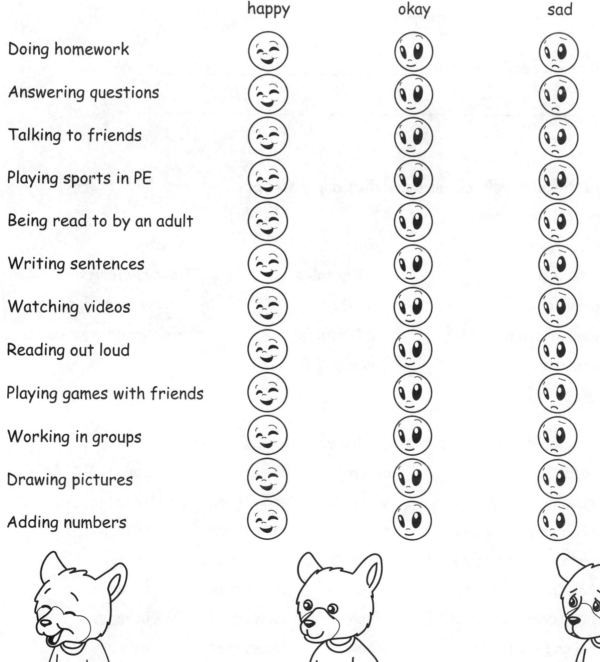

	happy	okay	sad
Doing homework			
Answering questions			
Talking to friends			
Playing sports in PE			
Being read to by an adult			
Writing sentences			
Watching videos			
Reading out loud			
Playing games with friends			
Working in groups			
Drawing pictures			
Adding numbers			

Name_____   Date_____

Sweet Activities

Use your favorite color to shade the things you like to do.

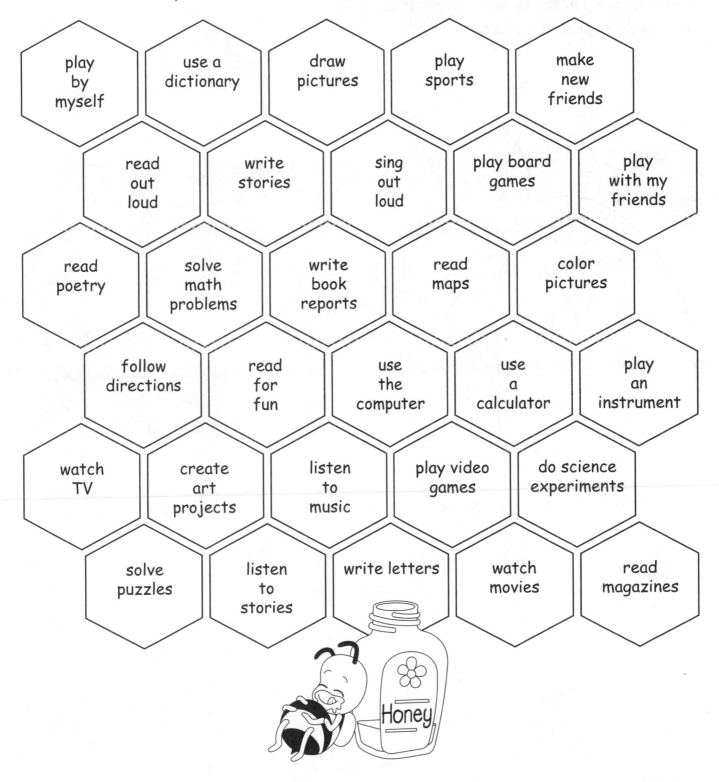

play by myself

use a dictionary

draw pictures

play sports

make new friends

read out loud

write stories

sing out loud

play board games

play with my friends

read poetry

solve math problems

write book reports

read maps

color pictures

follow directions

read for fun

use the computer

use a calculator

play an instrument

watch TV

create art projects

listen to music

play video games

do science experiments

solve puzzles

listen to stories

write letters

watch movies

read magazines

Honey

Name_____ Date_____

All About Me BEE...

Directions: Fill in the boxes with pictures and words to describe yourself.

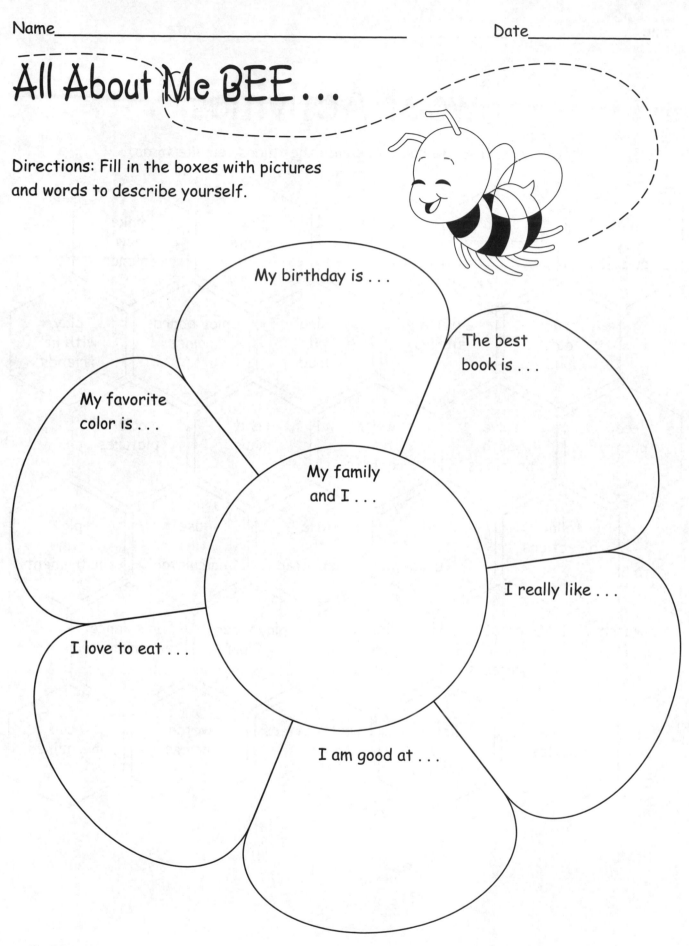

My birthday is . . .

The best book is . . .

My favorite color is . . .

My family and I . . .

I really like . . .

I love to eat . . .

I am good at . . .

16

Conflict Resolution ▪ CD-0306

The Important Things About Us

Meeting and making new friends can be difficult for some children. Incorporate literature, introduce the writing process, offer word processing practice, and provide an opportunity for students to learn about each other. Read the book *The Important Book* by Margaret Wise Brown to the class (HarperCollins Publishers, 1990). Discuss the language and repetitious pattern of the story. Model the pattern by creating a structure for each child to write their own "Important Things." Depending on the age and ability level of students, the structure could contain as few as three lines or as many as eight. After students type their drafts on the computer, use the rest of steps in the writing process to make sure they have written something they will be especially proud to add to the class book.

Instructions to give students:
"We are going to be using a word processing program to create *The Important Things About Us* for our own classroom publication.

Think about the pattern and repetition you heard in *The Important Book*. Now, we will write our own book following the same pattern. Before you go to the computer, you'll need to think about what is going to be on your page, using the information I've written on the board. Jot down your thoughts on a piece of paper (prewriting). Then, you'll take your notes to the computer and write (drafting). Your page should have five lines*."

Written on the board and said aloud.
"The first line should be:
The important thing about (your name)
is (a personal strength that you have).
The second line should tell about your family.
The third line should tell us something you like to do.
The fourth line should tell us about your favorite food.
The fifth line should repeat the first line."

*Note that these instructions are written for a five-line poem. The things that students "tell about" can vary.

Tell students to make sure that they have used the best words to explain what they were trying to say (revising). Then, help them to proofread for spelling, punctuation, and capitalization (editing). Have students print out their pages and illustrate them. Take a photo of the class for the front cover using a digital camera or use a scanner to add a photo. If you don't have access to this equipment, take a regular photo and paste it to the front cover of a binder. Add the pages to the class book and title the cover *The Important Things About Us*. Make this book available to share (publishing) by displaying it in a designated place in the classroom. Students will love to read about the "important things" about themselves and their peers.

The important thing about ashley is that she is kind.
She has two sisters and a dog named Buster.
She likes to swim and play with her friends.
Her favorite food is pizza.
But the most important thing about ashley is that she is kind.

The Important Things

About Us

Written and Illustrated by Mrs. Hughes' Class

Puppets

Show students how to make a puppet using a paper bag, sock, or panty hose. Supply yarn, markers, crayons, construction paper, fabric, and buttons for each student to make a face that represents herself. Remind students that the opening of the puppet should be at the bottom so that they can place their hands inside when the puppets are complete. Puppets are a handy tool to help shy students "talk" for them, while extroverted students will find the puppets a playful way to show their personalities.

Have students interview classmates using their puppets to ask the questions. As a class, brainstorm a list of interview questions. After students have interviewed one another, have them introduce each other to the class using the puppets. Be sure everyone gets to be the "introducer" and the "introducee." Puppet introductions provide a great forum to help students see the similarities and differences among each other. Students could also do a self-introduction using information from an interest inventory they have completed (see pages 11-16). Their puppets can do the talking as they tell about themselves.

Puppets can be used in many ways throughout the year. They provide a fun way for students to answer questions and for you to introduce new information.

Graphic Organizers

Graphic organizers provide another great opportunity for students to learn about each other and develop a sense of class community.

Venn Diagram—Have students work with partners to discuss their similarities and differences and write them in a two-column list. Then, draw a Venn diagram on the board. Have each student pair come to the board and fill in the Venn diagram showing what they discovered about each other.

Pictograph—As a class, determine the number of students in various categories, such as eye color, hair type, height, birthday months, hobbies, etc. Make a class bulletin board depicting this information using a pictograph.

Cloud Cluster—Another great display idea to illustrate the variety and similarities among your students is a cloud cluster graphic organizer. On chart paper, draw five to seven clouds. Brainstorm categories of information that students would like to learn about each other. Record the information in the clouds.

See pages 20-21 for examples.

How we are alike and different

Me

brown hair
like blue
E.T.
ride bikes
only child
June birthday
car rider
bring lunch

Katy

like dressing up
blue eyes
swimming
pizza
friends

My friend

blond hair
like pink
Stuart Little
roller skate
sister
April birthday
ride the bus
buy lunch

Elizabeth

All About Us

10 girls

9 boys

blue- 7
green- 2
brown- 10

hair color
black-4
brown-10
blond-3
red-2

curly 5   straight 14
7   12
short   long

Over 4' 10
about 4' 3
under 4' 6

January-3   March - 2   April - 1   May - 4
July - 2   September-3   November-1   December-3

Favorite Foods

hamburger	8
pizza	2
chicken	4
taco	4
hot dog	1

Favorite Snacks

ice cream	10
cake	3
cookies	3
popcorn	3

Favorite Sports

3 basketball   4 baseball

9 soccer   3 football

Favorite Colors

5 blue   3 green

4 red   2 purple

3 yellow   2 pink

Birthday Months

3 January	4 May	3 September
0 February	0 June	0 October
2 March	2 July	2 November
1 April	0 August	2 December

Centers with Small Groups

Listening Center

Classroom centers can be utilized to promote a positive classroom community. These specially designated places, where individual students or small groups can work quietly, provide a focused atmosphere for students to reflect. A listening center is the perfect place to start. Stock the center with songs and books on tape that promote friendship, understanding, and acceptance. See below for recommended titles. Place soft, washable pillows on the floor. Add headphones for listening to tapes. Have baskets of friendly books available for students to read and listen to each other. Invite parents as special scheduled guest readers for the listening center.

Recommended Titles:
- *It's Okay to Be Different*
  by Todd Parr
  (Little Brown Children's Books, 2001)

- *Why Do You Love Me?*
  by Dr. Laura Schlessinger
  (HarperCollins Publishers, 1999)

- *Mean Soup* by Betsy Everitt
  (Harcourt, 1995)

- *I Love You the Purplest*
  by Barbara Joosse
  (Chronicle Books LLC, 1996)

Post Office

Designate an area for students to write kind letters to classmates. Have envelopes, student "addresses" (students' seat locations), stationery, postcards, and "stamps" (stickers) available. Students can write letters or postcards and place them in a classroom mailbox made from a shoe box. To create the mailbox, remove the lid. Cut an opening into one of the short ends of the box by making a semicircle shape, beginning from the bottom of the box, arching toward the top and ending at the bottom. Leave the bottom side attached. This will serve as the mailbox door. Place the lid on and cover the mailbox with adhesive contact paper. Add a mailbox flag to indicate when mail is placed inside. By using a brad paper fastener, the flag can be moved up and down to indicate whether the mailbox contains mail. Classroom mail can be delivered by a designated student mail carrier. Read the class mail before it is delivered to prevent inappropriate notes.

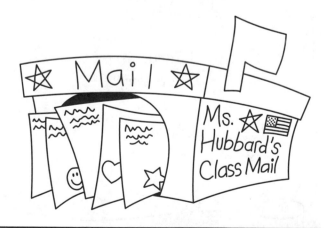

Computer Center

At the computer center, provide students with a topic. Using a word processing program, have students working at the center respond to the selected topic, such as "I am really good at . . .", "One thing I really want to learn how to do . . .", "Sometimes I feel . . .", "If I ran the classroom, I would . . .", "The best part about being me . . .", or "Friends mean a lot to me because . . ." Select topics that help you get to know students and how they are feeling. Since students work on each computer by themselves, you can also deal with sensitive issues by selecting topics that may include issues of divorce, loss, and arguing. Then, students can decorate their responses with computer graphics, stickers, crayons, or markers. A collection of responses can be stored in each student's individual portfolio.

Publishing Center

Stock the classroom publishing center with old greeting cards (holiday, congratulations, sympathy, birthday, etc.). Cut off and save the front covers (the side with the illustration and opening message). Encourage students to write their own messages and attach them to the illustration portion. Throughout the year, as various events happen, have students make personalized cards and send them to their friends, family, and classmates. Each month, you could have each student make a "Thinking of You" card to give each child within the classroom to make them feel extra special.

Specific School Card-Giving Opportunities:
- Get-well cards to sick student or school staff member
- Congratulations cards to other classes after a classroom performance or big event
- Thank-you cards after a school visit or field trip
- Holiday cards to other classes
- Birthday cards for the classmates, principal, and school staff members

Arts & Craft Center

Art is a great way for students to express themselves and their emotions. Provide materials and creative ideas, and watch their imaginations soar! It is important to give students project title ideas, written or picture instructions, sample projects, and books for specific ideas. Vary the activities, offer choices, and place value in the completed products so that students put their best efforts into their work.

Recommended supplies include:

watercolors	paper plates
glue	greeting cards
plastic cups	wallpaper books
paper lunch bags	yarn
washable markers	white paper
stickers	index cards
scissors	cloth scraps
construction paper	glitter
colored pencils	crayons
Easter grass	paintbrushes

Some art activity topic ideas:

How I Look	How I Feel
Feeling Happy	Good Thoughts
Best Friends	It's Funny When . . .
My Emotions	Angry Means _____
My Family	When I Get Mad . . .
The Saddest Day	

Music Center

Use the music center to reinforce topics that the class is working on. Utilizing songs familiar to students, show them how to change the lyrics to make a new class song. The lyrics should be about a social skill or specific area in need of attention. For example, Betty has a habit of taking things she finds and keeping them. To instill the importance of returning objects to their owners, begin by explaining why it is important to return things that aren't yours to keep. Then, teach the children a song about what to do when things are found in class. The next time this type of incident happens, sing the song together as a friendly reminder. Here's an example using the tune from "Old McDonald."

I have found a school supply, E-I-E-I-O.
And I must find its owner, E-I-E-I-O.
With a pencil here and a crayon there,
here's some glue, there's some glue,
does this item belong to you? E-I-E-I-O.

After writing songs as a class, have students write songs in the music center. Supply a list of topics. When students write a song, they can teach it to the class.

Familiar tunes to use:
- Row, Row, Row Your Boat
- This Old Man
- I've Been Working on The Railroad
- Twinkle, Twinkle, Little Star

Reading Center

Entice students to read friendly, positive literature by establishing a comfortable spot in a specially designated area in the classroom for doing nothing but reading! Pillows, a soft rug, carpet squares, stuffed animals, and beanbag chairs can help to create a cozy atmosphere. Surround the area with baskets of books, bookshelves, book character puppets, and of course, a selection of books to help send the message to children that reading is important! Be sure that your class library includes books that cover important issues, such as friends, self-acceptance, family, and emotions.

Recommended Reading:

- *When I Feel Angry* by Cornelia Maude Spelman (Albert Whittman & Company, 2000).
- *Glad Monster, Sad Monster* by Ed Emberly and Anne Miranda (Little Brown and Company, 1997).
- *A to Z, Do You Ever Feel Like Me?* by Bonnie Hausman (Dutton Children's Books, 1999).
- *L is For Loving* by Ken Wilson-Max (Hyperion Books for Children, 1999).
- *The Ant Bully* by John Nickle (Scholastic Press, 1999).
- *My Friend John* by Charlotte Zolotow (Random House Children's Books, 2000).
- *Different Just Like Me* by Lori Mitchell (Charlesburg Publishing, 1999).
- *The Loudness of Sam* by James Proimos (Harcourt Brace & Company, 1999).
- *Mary Louise Loses Her Manners* by Diane Cuneo (Doubleday Books for Young Readers, 1999).
- *I Feel Happy, and Sad, and Angry, and Glad* by Mary Murphy (Darling Kindersly Publishing, 2000).
- *Today I Feel Silly and Other Moods That Make My Day* by Jamie Lee Curtis (HarperCollins Children's Books, 1998).
- *Wemberly Worried* by Kevin Henkes (Greenwillow Books, 2000).
- *Don't Need Friends* by Carolyn Crimi (Doubleday & Co., 1999).
- *A Rainbow of Friends* by P. K. Hallinan (Ideals Publications, 2001).

Now That We're Friends

A Royal Good Time

Read *Princess Lily Goes to Camp*, by Katherine Cristaldi (Putnam Publishing, 1997) aloud to the class. This story is a delightful tale about a little girl who goes to camp and needs to be a better friend to the characters she meets. After reading the story, discuss what people do to be good friends. Ask students to brainstorm a list of "Good Friend Descriptions," and record the list on the board. Have students draw classmates' names to make a friend crown for them. Students can create an individual crown to give to the classmate it describes.

Here's how:

Enlarge, copy, and cut out the crown pattern for each student (see page 28). Have students decorate the crowns by gluing construction paper jewels accented with glitter. On each jewel, ask students to write one descriptive word that describes a friend (listed on the board). Have students give their crowns to the classmate whose name they drew. Since each student receives a crown, this activity shows that everyone possesses good friend traits. And, this gives students an opportunity to think about the wonderful friends that they have in the classroom!

Materials needed:

enlarged copies the crown pattern

colored construction paper cut into jewel shapes

glue

stickers

glitter pens

scissors

After the crowns have been given out, have students sit together in a circle on the floor while wearing their crowns. Ask students to share a time they can remember when they had fun being a good friend. Just like Lulu in the *Princess Lily Goes to Camp*, students will be encouraged to be good friends and appreciate the good friends they have.

After students wear their crowns, display them by stapling them on a bulletin board. If a student needs a subtle reminder during class, with eye contact and a simple point to the board, the child is easily reminded of the good traits he should be exhibiting.

Students "Reflect" on Good Friends

As a class, discuss what a good friend looks like. Do good friends have ears for listening, eyes for seeing how others are feeling, a mouth for saying kind words, a big, kind heart for showing kindness?

Provide each student a copy of the hand mirror pattern (see page 28) and a thin piece of chipboard or sturdy cardstock on which to trace the pattern. After cutting out the hand-mirror shape, have each student cut an oval piece of aluminum foil and glue it above the mirror's handle to provide the "mirror." Ask students to look at themselves in their mirrors and reflect on what kind of friends they are.

Tell students to think about what friendship characteristics each of them has. Are you a good listener? Do you use kind words? Do you consider other people's feelings? After students have thought about these questions, ask them to share their thoughts. Record student responses on the board. Next, have students draw a picture of themselves showing their good friends traits. Then, have them glue their illustrations to the aluminum foil on the mirrors. Display the mirrors to serve as positive reminders.

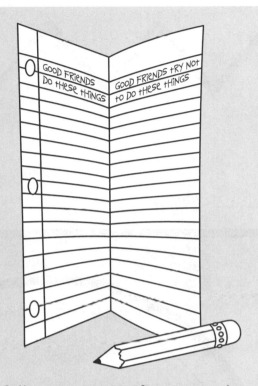

As a follow-up activity from your class discussion on reflecting on good friends, have students fold a piece of notebook paper in half vertically. At the top of the left column, ask students to write "Good Friends Do These Things," and on the other column, "Good Friends Try Not to Do These Things." Tell students to list the appropriate items in each column. After a few minutes, talk about what students have written down. Ask them which things they have done. Students will probably realize that they have done things from both columns. Discuss how it can be a class goal to do more of the "good things" and to avoid the "not to do" things. This activity can be a safe way to make students aware of behaviors that bother others. Remind students that we often forget to treat others the way we want to be treated.

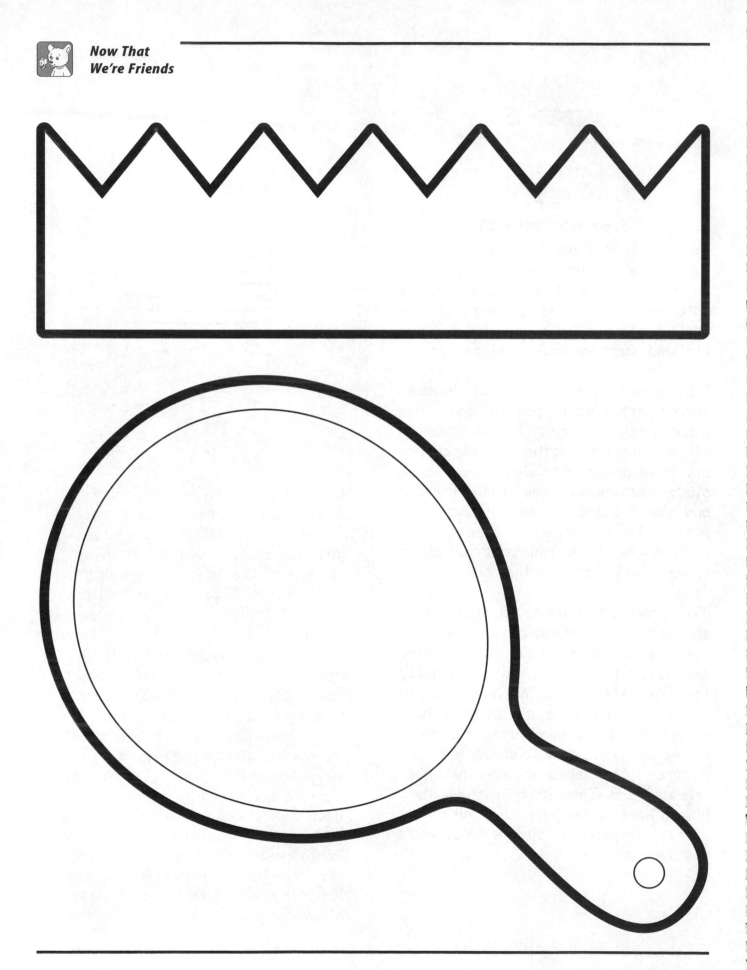

Kind Comments: Building Classroom Communication

Encourage Kind Acts

Compliment Hand-Outs

Build a positive classroom environment by encouraging students to offer positive feedback to each other. A fun way to do this is to prepare several paper hand-shaped cutouts, so that there are several for each student to "hand out" a kind compliment. Place the cutouts in a convenient place for students. Throughout the week, allow students to give a kind compliment to a classmate by writing something nice about the classmate on the hand cutouts. These compliments can be given to you to distribute or they can be "mailed" in the student mailboxes (see right) or Post Office center (see page 22).

My Mailbox

Have students make their own mailboxes for appropriate notes to each other. Have students cover empty tissue boxes or shoe boxes with construction paper or contact paper. Then, they can decorate them with markers, crayons, paint, stickers, and glitter. Student mailboxes can be placed on desktops, countertops, above cubbies, or placed in a classroom mail center. Make sure that each child has a mailbox with her name clearly displayed on the outside of her mailbox. Each week remind students to write and drop in their positive comments to each other. (Be sure to check students' mailboxes to ensure only appropriate notes are being shared.)

You're a Real Treat!

Invite students to make a compliment candy card to give a parent, faculty member, or special adult in their lives. Give each student a piece of 8 ½" x 11" sturdy cardstock. Have them fold the paper in half. On the inside of the card, help students write a thank-you for something kind the adult did for them. On the outside, students can write candy-related messages, saving room for the candy to be attached with tape. Students can be rewarded for their hard work by eating the extra candy!

Sample candy phrases: *You are so SWEET when you . . ., What a TREAT you are!, You were SUGAR and SPICE and oh, so nice when you . . ., Candy-BAR none—you are kind!*

"Catch 'em Being Kind"

Encourage students to say kind phrases to each other in the classroom and on the playground. Randomly "catch" students using kind, appropriate phrases. Compliment children for their choice of words and kind remarks, then place a marble in a classroom jar. When the jar is full, celebrate classroom kindness with ice cream, a class game, or other special treat.

This activity could be adapted to accompany and reinforce the math curriculum as well. Make a large pizza from poster board, cutting the pizza into pieces. Attach magnetic tape to the back of each slice. Each time you observe a kind act or hear a kind compliment, hang a piece of pizza on the chalkboard. Discuss fractions, how many pieces make the whole, identify the fraction of pizza filled in, and identify the fraction of pizza missing. Each time you catch a good behavior, hang another piece of pizza until the pizza is whole. Then, celebrate with a class pizza party!

Photos, Photos, Photos

Throughout the year, take pictures of students showing the many kind acts that occur in the classroom and playground. Place the photos in a class scrapbook, and with student help, add captions and decorate with stickers. This is a great class treasure to have available at conferences or on display during Parent's Night to share the positive activities and interactions that occur during the school day. Parents will enjoy seeing their children in a happy learning environment, interacting with classmates.

Students could also earn classroom minutes. Catch a student expressing genuine, kind words or making a kind act and add five minutes to a classroom clock display. Bring up various time facts, such as how many minutes are in an hour. When the class has earned thirty minutes, for example, discuss how many minutes are needed for a whole hour. After the class earns one hour, share a movie, free recess, or other extended class reward for treating one another with kindness. This way, two objectives are met—students realize the importance of kinds words and strengthen their time facts!

There are many other variations for these types of classroom incentives. Think about what type of educational objective you would like to teach and incorporate a "catch 'em being kind" motivator.

An Alien Exchange

You might find that some students need guidance on how to appropriately compliment each other and how to receive compliments.

Have students create fictional characters, such as aliens. Invite each student to draw a character and give it a name. Ask students to walk around the room with their alien picture held in front of themselves. As they walk around the room, prompt them to exchange compliments with their new alien friends. For instance, "I love your three yellow eyes!" and "Thank you, and you have nice green horns." Allow them time to be creative and to practice offering nice, fun compliments.

After the compliment-sharing opportunity, as a class, discuss how the aliens felt when receiving and giving compliments. Some students may offer words like good, kind, or nice. Other students may suggest that they questioned the honesty or sincerity of the compliments. Some may say that they felt their alien was being made fun of because it had three eyes or horns. All of these feelings and thoughts make excellent teaching moments, providing time for discussions on feelings, sincerity, and comment appropriateness.

Then, ask students to turn to the person next to them and provide an honest compliment. After this exchange, discuss how that experience made them feel. Ask students to give examples of compliments that they heard from their peers that made them feel good. Have students share what they said in response to the compliments. Throughout the school year, continue to invite the class to have moments of compliments! What started out as an alien exchange can come quite natural and normal, and students will learn how to give and receive kind words.

Kind Compliments

Allow students the chance to develop vocabulary, as well as compliment peers. Have each student cut a large heart shape from construction paper and decorate it with markers, glitter, and paper doilies. Pass out a class name list to each student. Instruct students to write a different kind word for each of their classmates next to their names. If appropriate, make thesauruses available for students to select specific words to describe their peers. Brainstorm words with younger students. Then, collect the hearts and class lists containing the complimentary words. Write each compliment on the owner's heart and return the special memento for each child to keep.

Helping Hands

Instead of being the watchdog for helpful behavior all the time, give students the opportunity to acknowledge it as well. Have students trace and cut out their handprint on colorful construction paper. Instruct students to write the name of a peer who has done something nice for them in the palm of the handprint. Tell them to use each finger to describe the kind deed and tell how they felt having such a good friend. Place the Helping Hands in a basket and read a few each day. Students can continue to add hands to the basket throughout the year. Hang up the Helping Hands on a bulletin board or create a border to keep up the positive momentum and to show off your kind, caring students.

Kind Compliment Game

Introduce students to the Kind Compliment Game. It is easy to make and fun to play. To make the game board, unfold a manila folder and lay it open on a tabletop. Place stickers or use markers to create a path from one side of the folder to the other, winding its way across the folder. Objects can be added to provide obstacles along the path (river, rocks, trees). Laminate the

Materials Needed to Play:
2 dice

2-6 different-colored craft pom-poms

manila folder

markers or stickers

board-game folder or cover with clear adhesive contact paper. To play, students roll the dice and move their pom-pom (their game piece) around the board game. Each time a player is finished with a turn, they must say a kind compliment to their opponent. Then, the other player does the same. This game objective is to be the first player to reach the end of the path. The game ends when all players make a closing kind compliment to another player. With this game, everyone is a winner!

Game-ending sample compliments:

Jon, you seemed to give the nicest compliments.
Donna, it was really nice of you to let Jennifer go first.
Hector, you were really good when you won the game. Thank you for not showing off.

100 Nice Things to Hear and Say

1. Good Work
2. Fantastic
3. I'm proud of you!
4. Hip-hip-hooray!
5. You do neat work!
6. Beautiful work
7. Right on target
8. Stick to it!
9. You're amazing!
10. Remarkable
11. Great start
12. Artistic
13. Marvelous
14. You figured it out!
15. Progressing nicely
16. Congratulations
17. Sensational
18. Keep on going!
19. Go for it!
20. Way to go
21. Well done
22. You did it!
23. Hooray
24. Great job
25. Keep on learning!
26. Awesome day
27. Excellent
28. That's the best!
29. Good for you
30. Thank you
31. Nice attempt
32. I believe in you!
33. You've got it!
34. Very Creative
35. Keep on going!
36. You made my day!
37. Wonderful work
38. You must be proud—I am!
39. Your hard work paid off!
40. I like the way you did that!
41. You are showing real talent!
42. You are showing growth!
43. You're a great person!
44. Three cheers for you!
45. I know you can do it!
46. What an improvement!
47. Very Creative
48. You improved!
49. Bravo!
50. Thank you
51. Outstanding
52. You make others proud!
53. Glad to know you!
54. We're lucky to have you!
55. Good going! What's next?
56. WOW
57. You made it happen!
58. I knew you could do it!
59. Keep trying!
60. Almost
61. Don't give up!
62. Sweet Success!
63. You are getting closer
64. I can count on you!
65. Super
66. Cool
67. You really shine!
68. Great discovery
69. I appreciate you!
70. Superb
71. You're hard working!
72. Progressing nicely
73. You are nice!
74. Thanks for helping today
75. Thanks for doing your best
76. What a great kid you are!
77. You are one of a kind!
78. You are a friend!
79. Way to go!
80. Thanks for being you!
81. You light up our room!
82. You made my day!
83. Phenomenal Feat
84. What an example!
85. Thanks for being your best!
86. I appreciate your help!
87. You did it!
88. You are awesome!
89. Kindness counts
90. Thanks for being honest!
91. I can count on you!
92. Awesome attempt
93. You were today's treasure!
94. Thanks for making my day!
95. Your made a difference!
96. What a super day you had!
97. I saw you sharing . . . thanks!
98. You made today special.
99. I caught you being good!
100. What a worker!

Sharing Circles

Sharing Circles can be a daily or weekly activity. They allow students a chance to work out conflicts, share feelings, and encourage positive actions. Sharing Circles also make a nice wrap-up to the last few minutes to bring positive closure to each day. Here are two ways to use Sharing Circles.

Caring Circle

Invite students to sit in a circle on the floor with their legs crossed. Begin the caring circle by gently placing your hand on the shoulder of the student sitting to your left. Then, say one nice, honest comment to that child. Next, it is that child's turn to say something to the person beside her. Then, he says something to the person to his left, and so on until the caring circle has gone all the way around the circle and back to the teacher. In place of the shoulder touch, you can also have students use a ball or stuffed animal to gently toss to the next student speaker. You can also use the caring circle to talk about classroom issues that arise. Once you've established that the caring circle is just that, a place to open up and share how much you like and appreciate each other, discuss frustrations and small conflicts that arise in the classroom. The caring circle provides a safe, comfortable forum for discussion.

Hug Rug Circle

Get a soft rug, large enough for a student to sit on comfortably. Place the rug in a designated place in the classroom. You can use this little "hug rug" for many purposes. Randomly select students to step on the hug rug or use it as a reward for students to earn the opportunity to visit. For example, if you notice a student is having a particularly tough day and recognize that it is due to her feeling left out, invite her to sit on the hug rug. Or, if a student has shown great improvement in spelling, ask him to sit on the hug rug. When invited to sit on the hug rug, classmates sit in a circle around the student. Then, the student can pick his hug rug reward, perhaps a hug, a smile, a high five, a handshake, or a pat on the back from his classmates. Discuss how these are ways that good friends let each other know that they care about them and appreciate who they are! This activity also gives you a chance to demonstrate appropriate touches and acceptable ways to provide praise. With this activity, consider children who are not used to being touched. Some students may need to be warmed up to the idea if they aren't accustomed to it.

Remembering Rules: Establishing Clear Expectations

Equal Opportunities

Special Helpers

It is important to create a tone of fairness when establishing classroom rules. Teachers are the model for appropriate behavior; therefore, it is vital to show that it is important to you that everyone is treated the same. It is easy to fall into the habit of choosing our "best and brightest" students for special jobs and present these students to others as examples to follow. While these top students certainly deserve recognition, so do all students. Also, there are some students who might be prone to make incorrect choices that might need our attention the most. Utilizing students that are not known for positive behavior can often help them. For example, teach a student, who is known to employ bully-type behavior, this week's computer lesson first, so she becomes the class expert. Then, have her show her classmates the new computer

Chip Cup

Another way to establish a sense of fairness in the classroom is to provide everyone an opportunity to participate equally when calling on students. It is important to make turns "fair." Assign each student a number and write it on a poker chip in permanent marker. Put the chips in a plastic cup and randomly pull each one out. To be sure everyone eventually gets a turn, leave the selected chips out of the cup until all the chips have been drawn. When the cup is empty, refill it with chips and start again. You can also write students' names on wooden craft sticks. Place the sticks in a can. Randomly pull the sticks from the can and read the names on the sticks.

skill. Often, bullying (as well as other undesirable behavior) stems from insecurity. As the student known for her bullying gains confidence, you might see some of those old, negative habits decrease. For a child who has difficulty making and keeping friends, allow him to be in charge of something important that involves positive interaction, such as the classroom librarian or errand runner. Choose a struggling reader to deliver daily announcements (or another responsibility that lets her be successful). By choosing kids who aren't normally selected, you model an important lesson in equality to your students, as well as help build the confidence of those who need it most! Allow every child an opportunity to share, participate, and have a turn. Soon you'll see all students as your best and brightest.

Go Fishing!

To continue developing an atmosphere of equality in the classroom, write students' names on poster board or cardboard, then cut them out in simple fish shapes. Laminate them or cover with clear contact paper for durability. Place the fish in a fish bowl. When you need to group students for games or projects and don't want feelings to get hurt, select someone randomly by going fishing! Place sticky tack on the back of the cutouts and attach them to a wall or board to display the cutouts in their groups. This provides an easy visual reference if the group activity must resume after lunch or the next school day. Students can also go fishing on their own when they need to select partners to run an errand or complete a partner task. This way, students won't feel pressured to pick others because it will be random. There are other variations for the fish, such as flower cutouts placed in a flower pot or apple cutouts placed in a wooden basket. For younger students who may not be able to read their classmates' names yet, place their wallet-sized picture in the center of the cutout so that students can recognize their classmates' faces until they can read their names.

Lining Up

Demonstrate that classroom procedures should be fair and fun! Put some pizzazz into the typical lining-up routine, while allowing different students to be at the head of the line. Instead of calling the quietest table to line up first, or just letting the class race to the door, try a different method each day. Announce, "If you are wearing orange today, you may walk to the door now. Next, the students wearing green can get in line." Keep announcing different categories, until each child has been identified and is in line. It's fun to end with something that includes all the leftovers and makes lining up fun and orderly. "Finally, anyone with hair may line up." Using a variety of techniques to get in line can prevent conflicts and establish orderliness. Vary the line-up categories throughout the week.

Other line-up categories include:
- birthday months
- hair color
- number of siblings
- unique features such as glasses
- wearing tennis shoes
- favorite activities
- book last read
- food choices in lunch boxes
- best subject
- middle name begins ends with ____
- favorite snack

Rule-Making 101

Your students may have an easier time accepting classroom procedures and rules if you take time at the beginning of the year to involve them in writing the discipline plan for the classroom. This process will foster ownership and will demonstrate to students how they contribute to the classroom climate and environment that they help create. Think of the following guidelines as you prepare to go through this process with your students.

1. Establish 4-5 rules.
2. Build in reasonable rewards and consequences.
3. Rules should be measurable and/or observable behaviors.
4. Rewards and consequences should fit the rules.
5. Change procedures and rules, as needed. For example, if students no longer need to be reminded to have materials ready for class, drop that rule and add one that deals with a classroom behavior that is proving troublesome.

There are some important rules that students may not suggest. As you develop and discuss the rules, you can "bring up" certain areas or rules. For example, in the first few days of school you are noticing that some students are not showing good sharing habits. During the classroom discussion on procedures and rules you can say, "I know how important sharing is going to be with all the great activities that we are going to do this year. Do you think we should incorporate that into one of our new class rules?" If students feel like it is being presented as a question and an option, they usually will agree with you.

Why Do We Have Rules?

As you begin making procedures and rules in your classroom, it is important to have a conversation with students about why we have rules at home and in our communities. Emphasize how rules help keep us safe by helping to establish order. Traffic rules are good to discuss because most children are familiar with them. Talk about what would happen if we didn't have stoplights, lines in the road, and speed limits. Why is it important that everyone understand these rules? What are the consequences for people who don't follow the road rules? What rules can we make to keep us safe and happy in our classroom? What rules can we make that will help us create a good place where we can learn? What would be appropriate consequences or rewards to go with our rules? Send a letter home to parents with the classroom plan for procedures, rules, rewards, and consequences that you and your students have developed.

Incentive Cards

Incentive cards are a good way to give children instant feedback on good behavior as students are learning the class rules. Attach a self-adhesive note, index card, or paper cutout to the corner of each student's desk. Each time a child meets the established, expected behavior goals for the day, place a sticker, stamp, or special mark on his card. When students earn a designated number of marks, they can earn a prize or special reward, such as a homework pass, pencil, or extra time in their favorite center. Of course, some students will need more frequent reminders and reinforcement. It can be helpful to connect the number of marks that students need to earn rewards that they have selected. For example, if you have a student who really likes dog stickers, on the back of the incentive card, write down his reward goal as dog sticker. When you observe the behavior getting off track, simply walk by the student's desk and flip over the card as a visual sign of the goal. Student motivation often increases if you allow the child to choose his own reward. Displaying a student list of prizes that you feel are acceptable will keep the rewards clear and reasonable.

A Note on Parents

If you have shared your classroom plan for procedures and rules with parents and made them feel a part of the classroom, they can be your best allies as you work towards improved behavior and work habits. In order to tap into this resource it is important to keep parents informed of progress and setbacks on a regular basis. You can do this with a simple daily or weekly behavior report that shows points earned for effort, behavior, and the quality and quantity of work done. If a child needs to work on a particular skill or goal it could be written on their incentive card (see left) and sent home each week. This will enable the parent to be a consistent part of their child's education and encourage their child's appropriate behavior.

If you think that a child's report needs more elaboration, write notes to the parent in the child's assignment book or journal to inform them of progress or setbacks. Paperclip the incentive card to let the parent see the reminder that the child has for his behavior. As a teacher, your time is very important and limited; however, a quick note when needed could provide a parent much appreciated feedback and an effective time saver for everyone involved in the student's development.

Ready Reminders

Making the rules is one job—following them is another. There are many good children's books to serve as helpful rule reminders. Read a story together that sets the scene for following rules. A great book to begin these discussions is *David Goes to School* by David Shannon (Blue Sky Press, 1999). Young David goes to school and is told "no" all day because he keeps breaking the rules. This story is a terrific springboard for a discussion on why we need to follow rules and how they help classrooms run smoothly.

Other great literature to review procedures and rules include:

Lily's Purple Plastic Purse
by Kevin Henkes (Greenwillow, 1996)
Lily brings her favorite items to school in her new purple plastic purse and has trouble remembering the classroom sharing rules.

Naughty Nancy Goes to School
by John S. Goddall (Margaret McElderry Publishing, 1999)
This wordless adventure is about a curious mouse who gets into a lot of mischief at school. Nancy wins her teacher over with a brave, kind act.

Take Turns, Penguin!
by Jeanne Willis (Carolrhoda Books, 2000)
This tale is about Penguin's first day of play school and the important lesson he must learn about sharing.

More titles to help build a caring classroom include:

- *We Share Everything* by Robert Munsch (Cartwheel Books, 1999).
- *When Sophie Gets Angry—Really, Really Angry* by Molly Garrett Bang (Scholastic, 1999).
- *Miss Nelson Is Missing* by Harry Allard (Houghton Mifflin, 1985).
- *Be Quiet, Parrot!* by Jeanne Willis (Lerner Publishing Group, 2000).
- *Chicken Soup for Little Souls* by Jack Canfield and Mark Victor Hansen (Health Communications, 1997).

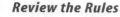

Progressive Story Starters

To review a classroom rule, use creative writing to get students back on track. Begin a language arts lesson by reviewing the main elements of a story: character, setting, problem, and resolution. Then, explain that small groups will work together to create a progressive story with a message. A progressive story starts with a trailing situation prompt written in a few sentences. One person writes a follow-up sentence to the sample prompt, then another student writes a related sentence, and so on until they complete the story. Provide students with a story prompt and title that coincide with the specific issue or rule that needs to be addressed and reviewed. You may have the groups work at the computer or with paper and pencil. Allow each student in the group five minutes to read what has already been written and write the next section of the story. Depending on how long you would like the activity to take, and considering the writing level of your students, you may choose to have them complete the process one to three times. Assign the last group member to be responsible for adding a solution or wrap-up sentence to the story. Completed tales can be illustrated and bound in a book to be placed in the classroom library. It is important to model the complete progressive story writing process as a class before having students work in groups. You can go around the room and write the story on the board and leave it posted for reference when students write their own stories.

Sample Situation Prompts

• Rule: Treat others as you want to be treated.

Carter, Maleek, and Sean live on the same street and used to sit on the bus together. A few weeks ago, Sean began hanging out with older boys on the bus. Now, instead of sitting together, Sean and his older group sit behind Carter and Maleek and tease them with mean names. Carter and Maleek now dread the bus ride home. Today . . .

• Rule: Be kind and respectful to everyone.

Miss Spencer just finished describing an important group project to the class and announced that she was going to assign work groups. Deana was unhappy when she found her group assignment. Not only was she stuck with Brandon, who sometimes smelled funny, but she also had to work with Brenda, who was quiet and wore ugly clothes. Deana . . .

• Rule: Be considerate of other people's feelings.

Bobby and Jake were best friends. They have been in the same class since kindergarten and used to spend weekends at each other's houses. Recently, Terrance moved next door to Blake. Terrance has become close friends with Blake. Jake knows the two boys are playing together while he is at soccer practice, and he is beginning to feel left out. Today, after practice . . .

Comic Strips

Another good way to provide reminders of classroom expectations involves using humor. Share several comic strip examples from the newspaper. Discuss how the words are written first, then the pictures are made to add more meaning to the comic strip. Then, write an original comic strip as a class using a recent classroom situation as the setting. Explain how writers often use comic strips to explain a point or tell a message. With your classroom rules displayed, divide students into small groups based on the number of rules you have. (For example, if you have four class rules, divide students into four groups.) Have students work together to create their own comic panels emphasizing a specific rule. The strips could demonstrate the benefits for following a rule or consequences for breaking it. Let students know that they should have fun with the comic strip, but that the point is to show that the rule is important. The illustrated comic strips can be displayed around the room or bound into a classroom comic book to be placed in the classroom library. By putting a humorous spin on classroom expectations, it not only lightens the heavy atmosphere that can build when discussing expectations and outcomes, but it also provides a friendly reminder as to why we have rules.

Bumper Stickers

Students love catchy slogans and often remember information better when using them. Provide each child with markers and a rectangular piece of sturdy cardstock, cut to 4" x 12". Brainstorm various popular slogans from TV commercials, magazine ads, and commonly seen bumper stickers. Have each student create her own bumper sticker with a well-recognized slogan for one classroom rule. Display the bumper stickers throughout the classroom. Soon students will use the catchy phrases to remind each other of the rules. If desired, encourage positive behavior and reminders of school rules by starting a school-wide slogan contest about responsible student behavior. Students could vote on the top three winners and have the winning slogans printed into real bumper stickers in school colors.

Be all that you can be...
Be prepared for class!

Limericks

There are many ways to incorporate writing into a review of classroom rules. Writing limericks is a creative way to do this. Begin by reading several together as a class. Discuss the rhythmic pattern and topics people have written about in limericks. Model the process by looking for rhymes, and then write your own together. Students or pairs of students can create their own limericks illustrating the pitfalls of making incorrect choices or rewards of behaving as they should based on class expectations.

There once was a bully named Sam
Who picked on a young girl called Pam.
He broke the class rule
Got in trouble at school
Just because he liked being a ham!

There once were a couple of lads
Who wanted the teacher to be glad.
They came into class
With a big, giant stash
Of candy to share with their friends!

There once was a teacher, Miss Burns
Who taught her nice class to take turns.
They worked hard together
Their manners got even better
Oh, how much fun it is to learn!

Classroom Brochures

Familiarize new students who enter class throughout the year with classroom brochures that have been designed by students. Brochures can be made with folded paper or created using a word processing program. Instruct students to include specific information about classroom expectations concerning procedures, rules, rewards, consequences, as well other information that they think would help a new student. Brainstorm a list of things that must be in the brochures. Tell students to think about what a student coming into the classroom would need to know to feel comfortable and a part of the class. When completed, these brochures will be helpful to new students and their parents. This activity also provides a wonderful, gentle reminder to your students who **should** already know the class expectations. Depending on the amount of time you want to devote to this activity, the class could design a more detailed school booklet and incorporate information about the school schedule, staff members, extracurricular activities, after-school information, and a school map. If you don't get many new students during the school year, these brochures could be placed on a welcome table for classroom visitors and Parent's Night.

Token Rewards

After classroom rules have been established (and reviewed as needed), reward positive behaviors as often as possible. This strategy reinforces the student's positive behaviors and showcases acceptable behaviors for students who need to improve. Taking the time each day to reward good behavior can save time and prevent small issues from becoming bad habits. Simple tokens like bingo chips or plastic figurines can be used as incentives for good behavior. Award them to students who exhibit desirable behaviors.

These tokens are inexpensive, so they should be given freely. Assign a value to them that enables students to exchange them for special privileges such as free time, a special trip to the library, time at the reading center or to play a computer game, or lunch with you or the principal. You could also set up a class treasure chest or class store, where tokens can be used to "purchase" pencils, markers, erasers, folders, stickers, candy, bookmarks, or inexpensive trinkets. You could establish a weekly trip to the treasure chest or store to build up the anticipation of collecting tokens. Parents are often very willing to donate towards your treasure chest or store, or you could see if funds are available through your principal or PTA group.

Don't Forget Incentive Cards!

Remember the Incentive Cards that you used to teach your classroom rules and procedures (see page 38)? Well, don't forget to use them to reinforce good behavior, too. Using Incentive Cards is a good way to give children instant and continuous feedback on their behavior (throughout the year, if needed). If you see that the Incentive Cards aren't as effective after a while, change the rewards. If you think that students should start moving away from the extrinsic motivation of the tangible rewards they get for good behavior, then talk to your students about how as we get older, "doing the right thing" is expected and that there are other kinds of rewards that we can get from doing what is right, such as pride, confidence, and self-esteem. If needed, you could still send home the Incentive Cards with students each week so that parents can be kept informed of their child's progress. Remember, if you start this means of communication at the beginning of the year, parents will expect to continue seeing it, so inform them if you are going to use a different method.

Keeping Contact

Continue to utilize parents throughout the school year. Keep them informed of progress and setbacks on a regular basis. You can do this with a daily or weekly behavior report that shows points earned for effort, behavior, quality and quantity of work done. The behavior reports need not be too elaborate. Most parents are pressed for time themselves. Incentive Cards offer a quick, reliable way to offer feedback (see page 38).

If you like to send parents feedback on a daily basis, sign off in the child's planner or assignment notebook. Draw a smiley face for a good day, or a question mark to indicate a not-so-good day. This will enable parents to be a part of the team to help bring about the desired improved behaviors in students.

Phone calls are a must for the parents of young elementary students. Even if you are employing a daily or weekly written contact method with parents, making regular verbal contact is important, too. Make it a personal goal to call two parents a day. These phone calls can be simple updates that children are doing well. Of course, there will be unscheduled phone calls as well. When calling a parent to report a setback in academic performance or behavior, be specific about classroom observations, listen to the parent, offer helpful suggestions, and make it clear that you want to see the child be successful. There is a good chance that the parent is frustrated with the same behavior at home. Let parents know that you are calling so that you can work together for a solution.

Throughout the year, it's important that you communicate not only about each child's academic growth to each parent, but also about the child's emotional and behavioral growth. Most parents are as concerned as you are that the best possible learning environment is available for students. Keep parents informed of the classroom expectations that you and your students establish at the beginning of the year.

Facing Feelings: Understanding Our Emotions

Emotion Exercises

Helping students to understand other people's emotions can be easier if you start by helping them identify their own feelings first. These activities give students an opportunity to think about what makes them feel safe and happy, and what makes them angry and hurt. They also reinforce the fact that we all get angry, and that it is okay to express those feelings in an appropriate manner. Understanding others and themselves helps children better approach others and recognize that everyone is unique.

Charades

Students may not realize that their faces and postures reveal their feelings. Explain to students that body language and facial expressions are essential tools in sending a message. Students can practice acting out these nonverbal signals by playing charades. Make cards with emotions labeled on them and place them in a bowl (see page 46). Allow each student to take turns selecting a card and demonstrating the emotion without using verbal clues. This activity will give students opportunities to see how different people look when feeling certain emotions. This also helps students recognize a classmate starting to get sad or mad and might prevent emotions from getting out of control in class.

Paper Plate Profiles

Give each student two paper plates. On one plate have them draw a picture of themselves when they look happy, and on the other when they look angry. Provide craft materials for the students to personalize their plates. Next, give each student two sentence strips. On one strip have them write and complete the phrase *When I am happy, I . . .* On the other strip ask them to write and complete the phrase *When I am angry, I . . .* Then, glue the plates back-to-back and attach the appropriate strip to the bottom of the plate. Suspend the plates from the ceiling using thread, so that students can recognize the faces as these two common emotions arise.

What to Do When You Get to 10

Children need to understand that everyone gets angry. It is important to also teach them strategies for dealing with anger. As an introduction to this concept, you might use the book, *When I Feel Angry* by Cornelia Maude Spelman (Albert Whitman, 2000). A simple checklist like the one on page 47 also provides students with strategies to handle anger.

embarrassed	happy	shy
tired	excited	angry
scared	hungry	disappointed
proud	nervous	relaxed
impatient	jealous	frustrated
lonely		hurt

What to Do When You Get to 10

When you get mad, it can help to talk about your anger with a friend or adult that you trust. There are other things you can do when you get angry, too. Look at the list below. Put a check mark in the box next to the things that have helped you when you've been angry. Then, think about the others on the list. Put a check mark in the box next to things that you would like to try the next time you are mad.

When I get angry I can . . .	I've tried it. It works!	I'll try it next time.
Count to 10 and take a deep breath.	☐	☐
Talk to a good friend.	☐	☐
Ride my bike or take a walk.	☐	☐
Run around outside in a safe place.	☐	☐
Sing my favorite song.	☐	☐
Draw or paint a picture.	☐	☐
Give someone I love a hug.	☐	☐

Two other ideas that I could try are . . .

1.

2.

One-On-One Role-Playing

Role-playing exercises are a great way for students to demonstrate various emotions. It is important to give children the opportunities to act out realistic situations in a risk-free environment. This activity allows students to express themselves, become aware of their own feelings and the feelings of others, and discuss acceptable reactions. After discussing why friends sometimes disagree and get angry, provide a written exercise for students to complete individually (see page 49). Then, let them express their thoughts verbally with partners. After students share one-on-one role-play with each other, as a class, discuss how tone of voice, facial expressions, and body language can be interpreted in different ways.

Explain that the "I-Feel-Messages" (like those they completed for the one-on-one role-play on page 49) are a good way to appropriately share their feelings directly. If they use these messages, they can often help a potentially bad situation become a healthy, friendly conversation.

Role-Playing Cards

Role-playing can also provide sample situations to help students acquire the necessary assertive skills to communicate their feelings, wants, and needs without being confrontational. It also gives them the chance to see social exchanges modeled appropriately. Sending a clear message is an important part of communicating emotions. Students need practice and instruction doing this, as well as responding to these messages correctly.

Prepare role-playing situations cards (see page 50). Group students in pairs. Provide time for them to work together to develop a dialogue about one of the situations. Then, allow the pairs to role-play in front of the class. Classroom discussions should follow each scenario. Talk about other ways to handle each situation. Also, point out how "I-Feel-Messages" can set the tone for the encounters when/if they were used in the role-play. These cards provide a sampling of social situations that may occur. To make this activity even more meaningful, allow students to create their own problems and solutions that they have encountered at school and home. Working on real-life situations not only provides students insight on how to handle real conflict, but it also gives you a chance to see what is going on in their world.

One-On-One Role-Play

Sometimes people don't know that what they are doing bothers you. You have to tell them. Take a moment to think about a situation when you were angry or upset with a friend. Fill in the blanks in the conversation below.

A. I am angry/upset because you _____

_____ . I feel _____

when you do that. Next time, I hope you _____

_____ .

B. I am sorry that I

_____ .

I didn't mean to make you feel

_____

Next time I will try to

_____

You and two classmates are friends. Lately, though, they haven't let you play with them during recess. How do you feel? What will you say to your friends?

Your friend has changed lately. He has begun to make bad choices. You still like your friend, but you don't agree with his decisions. What will you do about this friend?

Someone in your class begins to call you silly names. It may be fun to them, but you don't like it. How do you feel? What will you do?

A classmate in your group never takes turns. She always wants to be first and usually gets her way. How will you handle it?

A classmate continues to "borrow" your supplies and other things without your permission. How do you feel about this? What will you do?

You brought a new toy to play with during recess. A classmate wants to play with it, but you haven't had much time to play with your toy yet. What will you say?

A friend of yours likes to talk about herself and her belongings. It seems like bragging to you. How does it make you feel? What will you do or say?

Every time you begin to speak with your class group, a member interrupts you. It seems like you aren't getting to speak. How does this make you feel? What will you say to your group?

Your friend is telling stories lately that seem really hard to believe. You think your friend may be lying to impress people. How does this make you feel? How will you handle your friend's behavior?

You and your friend are not playing together anymore. She doesn't talk to you as much as she used to, and you notice her choosing other partners in class. How does this make you feel? What will you do?

Preventing "Real" Problems

If you find that a student has problems dealing with his emotions appropriately, what do you do? For example, you've gotten several reports from different students that Jacob is calling them names. After investigation, you discover that he is exhibiting this behavior. You've followed your classroom rules and consequences and tried some strategies to help him stop this behavior, but Jacob has been inconsistent with his improvement. You've called his parents to explain the situation, and they told you that their son had this same problem in his class last year. What can you do to help reinforce the idea to Jacob that this type of behavior is never acceptable? Try using a contract with Jacob to identify the problem and offer a strategy to solve it. Schedule a conference with Jacob and his parents to come in and discuss the events you've experienced with him. Explain to him and his parents that you are aware Jacob is often a nice student, but the name-calling is not acceptable in the classroom. Use a contract to identify everyone's role to help Jacob improve his behavior. Mom's job might be to call you once a week to see how he did. Dad's job might be to talk to Jacob when he picks him up from school to see what kind of day he had. Jacob's would be to memorize the classroom rule about using a kind voice and call people by their real names. Your job, as the teacher, could be to give Jacob positive feedback when you hear him interacting appropriately with students. You can assign points that Jacob can work towards. Factor in a reward for Jacob when he is successful. You and the parents can decide if an incentive will be given at home or school. Give Jacob some time to show success.

If you find that the contract doesn't work, you may want to schedule another conference and make changes to the contract. They are great for documenting the strategies that the parent, student, and teacher have all agreed upon to help the student improve in a particular area. Using a contract also sends the child the message that you are all working together to help the him be successful. It doesn't place the entire responsibility on the child (which can be overwhelming), and it makes the parents aware and directly a part of solutions.

Each contract you write will need to be tailored to fit the student (see page 52). It will save time and make your contracts more consistent if you make one on the computer with a simple format and adjust the wording according to each situation.

Let's Work on This.

Date: _____

_____ is working on the
(student's name)

following skill/area: _____

	Super	Good	Needs Work
Mon.— _____	2	1	0
Tues.— _____	2	1	0
Wed.— _____	2	1	0
Thurs.— _____	2	1	0
Fri.— _____	2	1	0

_____ earned_____ points this week.

Based on the goals agreed upon, this week _____ DID/DID NOT
make an effort to meet his/her goals.

Student's signature _____

Parent's signature _____

Teacher's signature _____

Often "bullies" hurt people physically or emotionally because they do not know how to express their frustrations and emotions appropriately. "Bullying" is unkind behavior toward others that makes them feel scared, threatened, or defenseless. Many students deal with bullies on a regular basis. Most bullying occurs at school during non-structured activities such as recess, lunch, or dismissal time. Some might view bullying as "kids being kids," but many others feel that when adults fail to intervene this type of behavior is reinforced. When we don't intervene with bullying behavior, we fail to foster a caring learning community, and we send the message that bullying is acceptable. Students need to know that there is a "zero tolerance" policy for bullying because school is a place where everyone should feel safe. This subject requires direct discussion with students. Students need to be taught how to recognize what bullying behavior is, what options they have when faced with a bully, and how to develop a plan of action for victims of bullies, as well as those who see others being bullied.

Posting Options

Ask students to think about a time when they were teased at school. Give them time to describe that event in their journal and write how they felt and what actions they took. Next, ask students to list some possible actions they can take the next time they are confronted with teasing or bullying. Generate a class list and then as a group, create a poster that lists the choices you've agreed upon.

Happy Endings

Read the story *Thank You, Mr. Faulker* by Patricia Polacco (Putnam Publishing, 1998) aloud to the class. Discuss how the character in the story must have felt as she was being teased by the other students. Ask students to brainstorm a different ending to the story. For example, what if Mr. Faulker had not stepped in? What are some other possible endings for the story? Perhaps a friend stepped in or maybe the character confided in another adult for help. List the students' responses on the board.

BULLY-FREE ZONE!

If a bully is bothering you . . .

1. Tell an adult.
2. Tell a friend.
3. Tell the bully to stop.
   "Please stop. That hurts my feelings."
4. Ignore the bully by not reacting.
5. Avoid the bully.

Taking It Seriously

To establish the best learning environment in your classroom, you must establish a "zero tolerance" policy for bullying. Reports of bullying must be taken seriously. You can reinforce the idea that everyone has a role in creating an environment where teasing, name calling, and bullying are not permitted. Establish a procedure that holds everyone accountable. Sometimes bullying victims are hesitant to step forward, especially if they think nothing will be done or if they think their report will result in worse bullying. By giving students a chance to put the incident in writing, you can accomplish several things:

1. You establish written documentation that may indicate a pattern of behavior for either the bullies or the victims.
2. You give the students involved the opportunity to present the event from their own perspectives.
3. You send a message that the incident is important, and you want to find a solution.
4. You let all students know that anyone can report an incident of bullying and remain anonymous (if preferred). See page 55 for samples of bullying incident reports.

More Role-Plays

Give students an opportunity to "practice" healthy confrontations with bullies. Divide the class into small groups. Provide each group with a bullying scenario on an index card and let them work in small groups to role-play the interactions as short skits for the rest of the class. Be sure to allow time for discussion following each skit to give students a chance to reflect on the activity and share other strategies.

Some situations might include:

An older child teases your little sister at the bus stop. He calls her mean names. What should you do?

On the bus, a student takes your lunch money every day. He tells you that you'll be sorry if you tell on him. What should you do?

You have two friends that you hang out with. Lately, one of them has been mean to the other friend in your games and activities. What should you do?

Your teacher has assigned small group projects. One bossy student sits back, telling everyone what to do and threatens each member to earn him a 100. What do you do?

At recess, Sally took a toy that you and your friends are playing with. You have tried to ignore her, but she continues to take things from you. What do you do?

Dear _____ :   INCIDENT REPORT-A

Today _____ happened with _____ .

Where _____

When _____

Witness _____

My name _____

_____ Please don't tell _____ that I reported this.

_____ You can tell _____ that I reported this.

I am willing to sit down and discuss this with _____

_____

to prevent it from happening again. (list names of students or school staff members)

- -

Dear _____ :   INCIDENT REPORT-B

I need to speak to you. I want your side of the story, so please bring this report so that you can fill it out as we discuss this together.

Thank you,

Describe the incident.

_____

How do you think that made your classmate feel?

_____

What were you trying to accomplish?

_____

What do you think would be the right thing to do now?

_____

What would a better choice be in the future?

_____

Books on Bullies

Children's books to help prompt discussion and begin activities about bullying behavior include:

King of the Playground
by Phyllis Reynolds Naylor
(Aladdin Paperbacks, 1994)
Every day when Kevin goes to the playground, he is confronted by Sammy who claims to be the "King of the playground." Kevin discusses this problem with his father and finally gains the courage to face Sammy and the problem.

Bully Trouble by Joanna Cole
(Random House Publishing, 1989)
Arlo and Robby are best friends. When confronted with a bully at school, they discover how they can deal with him through the support of one another.

Documentation is Essential

Despite the most careful planning and preventative classroom strategies, you will likely experience conflicts in the classroom. Students will have varied strengths and areas that need improvement when interacting with others. Student contracts can help (see page 51-52); however, even more thorough documentation is essential to identify those students who may need more individual attention if the behaviors look like they are headed for a more serious problem, such as bullying. Keeping a simple checklist can be a beneficial resource when addressing specific problems that have the potential to become major issues. Note the date of each observation of the poor behavior, consequence and/or referral so that identifying patterns of problem areas and finding solutions to help the child and the parent is easier (see page 57).

The Ant Bully by John Nickle
(Scholastic, Inc., 1999)
Bullies usually pick on people smaller than them. So when Sid picks on Lucas, Lucas looks for someone smaller to pick on. He uses his squirt gun to pick on the ants, until an ant wizard shrinks Lucas to ant size, and he goes to work with other ants in the colony.

Mean Soup by Betsy Everitt
(Harcourt, 1992)
When Horace has a bad day, his mother teaches him how to deal with his negative feelings. She puts a pot of "mean soup" on the stove and lets Horace add his anger to the pot.

Behavior Documentation Form

Student Name:

Area of Concern:	Parent contacted	1st strategy used:	2nd strategy used:	Referred to counselor/guidance	Conference with parents	Other strategy:

Caring Community: Creating an Inviting Atmosphere

Door Decorating

Door Decorating

The atmosphere that you create in your classroom should reflect your efforts of creating a positive, caring environment. The classroom should be inviting to both classmates and visitors. A sense of community begins at your classroom door. Introduce students and build class pride by displaying photographs of each child on the door. Framing each picture with decorative shapes, such as stars or hearts, will add a positive touch to accent them. Also, have students decorate special shapes and hang them along the ceiling of the hallway to provide a welcoming path into your classroom. Banners and posters with positive messages taped to the hall walls and door also provide wonderful signs to display a positive message. You can also change your door and entry way to suit the various seasons, holidays, and other special occasions. Snowmen and gingerbread are perfect for winter, while bugs, flowers, and kites work for spring. However you choose to decorate it, your classroom door hallway may be the first impression you make on students and parents. Decorate the door so students and visitors look forward to entering your inviting classroom!

Bulletin Boards

One of the first things people will notice inside the classroom are bulletin boards. There are ways to make this decorating task easy and practical. Designate one board for each classroom need, such as a seasonal/thematic work display, class recognition, monthly calendar, classroom job assignments, and subject area information. This way, you are not forced to change every bulletin board with each new season.

However you divide up your bulletin board space, make sure that most of the bulletin board and wall space shows student work samples. By creating a simple title, adding a cute character, and displaying kid-created projects and papers, you help each child feel a sense of pride and belonging in your classroom. To make individual work stand out and to add color and vitality to the boards, frame each piece of work with a bright piece of construction paper or place a cutout shape in the corner of each student's paper. It is exciting for students to look at their work and reflect on the learning that occurred when they made a certain picture, took a certain test, or designed a certain project. Also, having the students' work displayed sends the message that their work is important and valued.

Even if you have each students' names posted on your door, be sure to also have a bulletin board that displays each class member's name together as a class for a class recognition bulletin board. Whether you use commercially made accents or create your own, you can inspire a feeling of belonging and pride in students if they see themselves as a team. Writing students' names on construction paper baseballs, basketballs, and footballs with a bulletin board title that says "We're on the Same Team in Ms. Gamble's Class!" is a simple way to show togetherness and establish a positive, caring work environment. You can also show the similarities and differences of students on a bulletin board by posting different characteristics. Design a "Three Cheers For . . ." bulletin board, featuring information about the many accomplishments that students have made in class (see page 60).

You can also feature a specific student each week to recognize every child. This provides an opportunity to point out the positives about everybody in your classroom. Cut out a large photograph background frame from a piece of white poster board. Add the title "ALL ABOUT." Add a place for the student's picture and name, then make four or five color blocks cut from construction paper. Have the class brainstorm some great characteristics that feature the student and write them on the color blocks. Place these around the student's "photograph" and display on a bulletin board to help instill self-worth and positive attention each week for every special child in your classroom (see page 60).

Three Cheers For...

Michael — Sharing books

Betsy — Improved spelling

Carol — Cleaning shelves

Juan — Following directions

All About

Favorite Book: Maniac Magee

Favorite Movie: Bambi

Favorite Food: Pizza

Kaitlyn Colleen

Hobbies: Soccer

Favorite Pet: Kitty

Best at: Dancing

BLUE

Favorite Color: Blue

Besides doors and bulletin boards, there are other great ways to use displays to show that the classroom is a place of positive learning. The first thing to consider when planning your classroom displays is what you want to achieve. Most likely you want to welcome students, parents, and other visitors. You probably also would like to instill a sense of pride and create the feeling that the room belongs to every class member. As with the bulletin boards, you can more easily cultivate a warm, friendly environment by focusing on students and their work.

Cubbies and Lockers

Whether they are located in the class-room or the hallway, student lockers and cubbies offer another great display area. Children can create monthly identification tags, complete with names or photographs. These decorations can be content-based, student-designed, or seasonal. Person-alized tags and coordinating colors show a sense of team and belonging.

Checking Your List

A checklist will provide a convenient tool for making sure all students' work is dis-played in the classroom. An example of everyone's work on the same project doesn't need to be displayed as long as each student has some work displayed. For example, display ten successful spelling papers, five excellent art projects, four model homework assignments, and six nicely written poems—until everyone has something hanging in the room. For some projects, you may decide to display samples of each student's work, but the checklist ensures that everyone has at least one item displayed—not just the "A+" work.

Beyond the Classroom

Don't limit welcoming displays to the classroom. Utilize empty, high-traffic areas where you take students daily. Think about walls that students stand along while waiting in the lunch line or doors that lead out to the playground area, and the lobby area of the school. You can also contact the school's board of education office and ask if they would like to display students' work in their offices or hallways. Many people within the school's community, such as the local library, might be interested in displaying projects and students' published books. Even the local fire department, police department, post office, and restaurants might enjoy having students' work displayed. This not only promotes a real sense of commu-nity outside the classroom walls, but also provides students a chance to truly publish their work!

Clotheslines

There may not be enough wall space to include all of the wonderful student work samples and positive messages that you would like to help make your classroom cheery. String rope or yarn from your ceiling and use clothespins to hang student samples. Using the clothesline not only affords more space, but it also brightens up a corner and makes the room more child-centered. Right above and below the chalkboard is the perfect place to hang a favorite quote or inspiring message for the class.

Book Displays

Create a special place in the room to display books with lessons that promote caring. By designating a specific place for these books, you not only provide a helpful mini-resource center for students, but you also send a message that literature has a priority in your classroom. If you don't have enough room for a designated reading center (see page 25), display the books on space-saving book racks or in sturdy baskets. Make sure these books are in good shape with the inviting covers showing. If you notice that there is a particular area where your students need a reminder, such as sharing, have several different titles available. Visit the school and local libraries often in order to keep the display fresh with new books.

Sharing the Spirit

With the classroom and school-wide student displays, you will share the positive energy throughout school. Encourage other teachers to show their classroom pride along the hallway wall space. That way, every class can have a part in making the school more attractive, child-centered, and positive! Near the school entrance, have information-only bulletin boards, with school-wide events and handouts available. Each grade level could have a designated area to post permission slips, important dates, and reminders for parents who visit the school. Your PTA might help by overseeing these school-wide displays, paying special attention that the information is current and available. After using these informative boards for a little while, parents will get used to stopping by them to get much of the information that they need. Encourage other teachers to contact local businesses and organizations in your community to display work from students (see Beyond the Classroom, page 61). You can further broaden the sense of community outside the school walls!

Shaping-Up Fun

Outline and cut out several large, simple school-themed shapes, such as a yellow school bus or a red schoolhouse. Trim the photographs so the students appear to be peeking out of the windows. Three or four head-and-shoulder photos can be cut to fit into each window. Use other simple shapes to capture class events and field trips, such as train cars, showing the students traveling to the zoo field trip. Students and parents will love looking at these creative creations and recalling the wonderful learning experience that you shared together!

Flower Frames

You can also use each child's school photo to create a flower. Each student can place his picture in a round center and add paper petals around it. Glue the flower-framed picture to a wooden craft stick. "Plant" each child's flower in a large flowerpot filled with plastic foam and cover with green craft grass or dirt. Display the flowerpots on a table or your desk.

Memory Board

Create a memory board using snapshots of your class at work and at play and ticket stubs and other small mementos from field trips. Cover a large piece of cardboard or foam board with a cheery fabric. Design a matrix with coordinating strips of ribbon and hot glue the ends to the back of the board. Hot glue each intersection of ribbon. Place snapshots and mementos under the ribbons. The ribbons will hold the photos in place. Display the memory board on an easel or chalkboard tray for all to see students learning and working together.

Framing Opportunities

There are many ways to use photographs for eye-catching displays. Proudly show off students using pictures taken at school or brought from home. A simple and effective way to proudly exhibit students is to take various student photographs and place them in different picture frames and prominently display them throughout the room. These framed memories create a sense of home in the classroom.

Bonus Box

Bonus Box

Another great way to recognize and encourage good examples of your students working well together is by making a Bonus Box. Get an empty paper box or large shoe box. Cover it with wrapping paper, adhesive contact paper, or wallpaper scraps. Then, decorate the box with buttons, glitter, construction paper cutouts, markers, and stickers. Label the box "Bonus Box." Place the box near your desk before students arrive on the first day of school so that they are inquisitive and excited about the box and its possible contents.

Explain that the Bonus Box is just that—a "bonus"—extra rewards for students who are working hard and are making noticeable improvements. This box can be used differently depending on your classroom needs and objectives, and also depends philosophically on how you feel about giving tangible rewards and incentives.

No matter how you use your Bonus Box, it is sure to encourage positive behaviors in your classroom! Be sure that each child gets a chance to visit it. No matter how you decide the box can work to best suit your classroom needs, the box will be special if it is treated with respect and with thoughtful kindness by both students and you. See page 65 for a fun Bonus Box Game.

Some Bonus Box Suggestions:

Give students who have made "good choices" or who contribute positively a ticket that can be completed with their name and the date, then placed in the Bonus Box. Have a class drawing once a week to randomly select student tickets and provide them with a simple reward to promote their kind acts.

Fill the Bonus Box with fun treasures, such as erasers, pencils, stickers, candy treats, certificates, or cards with fun tasks to complete. When students are caught doing extraordinary helpful or kind acts, they can select an item from the box.

The Bonus Box can be used to help find solutions to issues and conflicts that students have. Students can anonymously complete a form that provides space to share their concern. Concerns can be placed in the Bonus Box when they arise and at the end of the day, the teacher can share the concern with the class if appropriate. The student that offers the most helpful suggestion to the issue gets to select an item from the Bonus Box, which can be filled with little treasures (see suggestions in activity above). This way, solutions are being provided in a helpful way, there is recognition for positive problem-solving, and dealing with problems in a constructive manner is encouraged and rewarded.

Make a fun game from the Bonus Box! Copy several of the situation cards on page 66. On the blank sides of the cards, write several sample situations of behaviors that students need to work on. For example, if you notice that students are calling each other names on the playground, write a situation on a card (using made-up names).

Jerri is playing hopscotch with Susan and Micah. Jerri has not played this game very much, so she keeps stumbling. Susan keeps whispering silly names about Jerri, like "goofball" and "clumsy girl," during Jerri's turn. What would you do if you were Micah?

You can place students on teams or select students randomly. The object of the game is to give an appropriate solution to the given situation on the card. For each student's turn, she must draw a situation card from the Bonus Box and read it out loud (depending on the age of students, you may choose to read the card aloud). Then, the student must give her answer to the situation presented. Since these are open-ended questions, with several "answers" to the problem, you must decide if the response is appropriate. If the student's response offers a positive end to the situation or at least diffuses a potentially difficult situation, the student writes her name on the back of the situation card (which becomes an award ticket) and returns it to you. As tickets are given to you, place them aside until the end of the game. (If a student gives an inappropriate response to the situation card, you might decide to give her a chance to rethink and restate her original answer.) After everyone has had a chance to earn an award ticket, give the team who answered the most cards correctly a group reward or privilege, such as being the first group to line up to go to lunch that day. For the grand prize winner (which can be selected from either team if you choose to play this way), place all of the award tickets back in the Bonus Box. Pick one award ticket at random from the Bonus Box, which can be redeemed for a special prize, such as a free homework pass or sticker pack.

Situation Cards

Yahoo for You!

Name _____

Way to Go!

Name _____

You're Awesome!

Name _____

What a Great Friend!

Name _____

You're So Sweet!

Name _____

I'm Proud of You!

Name _____

Excellent!

Name _____

You're a Star!

Name _____

Some specific activities that can promote family participation and create a classroom environment that is inviting to all include:

- student work displays
- subject area presentations
- study skills sessions
- puppet shows
- poetry and music recitals
- plays and skits
- open houses
- guest readers
- parent/teacher conferences
- subject area fairs
- student art exhibitions
- star student recognitions
- family-friendly video premieres

Parent Participation

Invite the parents of students into the classroom to let to let their children know that school is an integral part of their lives and a place other than home where they are supported and cared for. Many times it is not possible for working parents to come to events scheduled during the day. Be creative and flexible with the times events are scheduled so that parents can attend at least a few throughout the year. When possible, schedule events during the school day, right after school, and in the evening. For those parents who are not able to attend, try videotaping presentations or informational meetings. Then, provide the class with a sign-out sheet so students can check out the video to take home. If you know how (or have a willing parent who can), create a Web page that uses digital photos to highlight student activities and display class information.

Backpack Connections

Establish a positive home-school connection by designing a series of backpacks, one for each aspect of the classroom community. Pack each backpack with a book or two about a particular topic that students are working on, an explanatory letter to parents on what is in the backpack, a stuffed animal to hug and read to, a few related simple follow-up activities with all materials, and a journal to record responses about the experience. Include topics such as equality, teamwork, respect, rules, bullies, friendships, and self-confidence. Introduce each backpack to students with enthusiasm. Rotate each pack through the class, giving each child a few days to complete the activities with their families and return them. Display completed activities in a special area in the classroom to maintain enthusiasm and show the importance of this project.

Constructive Communication: Talking About the Tough Stuff

Active Communication Activities

If you've established a positive, open environment with students, talking about more difficult topics can be much easier. Even if you have created a kind community, there are tough topics that children might be hesitant to discuss. Here are some ways to bridge that communication gap.

More on Role Playing

Sticking up for yourself without upsetting others is a delicate balance and a very tough lesson to teach, even for adults. There is a way, however, to express hurt, confused, angry, or jealous feelings without alienating people in the process. Let students role-play this important communication skill. Role-playing scenarios to empower students to be both assertive and mannerly provides students real practice. Before giving the scenarios to students, review using "I-Feel-Messages" (see page 48). Copy and cut apart the role-playing suggestions on page 69. Allow time for pairs of students to create a response for each.

Bring out the Puppets

If you introduce puppets to students early in the year (see page 19), they will be more comfortable using them to talk about difficult social lessons. Using the puppets to talk for them takes some of the pressure off the student from talking "in person."

Classroom Mailbag

Students need an anonymous outlet to place their requests to talk about some issues, so designate a Classroom Mailbag for these serious concerns. Talk with students about what types of subjects you want to address with the mailbag. Let them know this is for social concerns and conflicts (for example, not to ask homework questions). They should concentrate on the three F's—friends, feelings, and friction—when using the mailbag. It is vital to assure the children complete privacy with the mailbox. Use the problems found in the mailbag to stimulate conversation in a variety of ways. Begin by using the situations in a role-playing exercise, open the discussion in your Sharing Circle (see page 34) with the student's problem, or make the concern a journal topic for the day. Write your own concerns if you see conflicts arising in the classroom and to encourage students to utilize this tool.

How can you tell someone who cuts in front of you that you were first in line?

What can you say to a classmate who is telling silly jokes about you to make others laugh?

How can you ask to join classmates already playing a game at recess?

How can you tell a classroom neighbor to stop taking your supplies?

How can you tell a friend you would rather play with someone else?

What do you say to an older student who is picking on you?

What can you say to a classroom neighbor who keeps looking at your assignment?

What can you say to a friend when you haven't been honest with them?

How can you tell a friend that you don't like it when she copies your hairstyle and clothing?

What can you say when you haven't been a good friend to someone?

What can you say to a classmate you've been picking on?

What do you do when a friend apologizes to you after hurting your feelings?

What can you say to a friend who likes your ideas about artwork and writing so much that he uses yours instead of his own?

Modeling Appropriate Behavior

The Teacher-Model

Don't underestimate the effect your behavior has on students. In some cases, you spend more time with students than anyone—even their parents. In a sense, you

The ABCs of Modeling Appropriate Behavior

Act how you want your students to act.
Be mindful of your tone of voice.
Consider what you say to others.

are on stage, and your every action and word are being observed and often modeled by students. If you doubt this, watch students at play on an indoor recess day; you will likely see and hear them saying some things that you say and using mannerisms that you do.

If you want your students to be more polite, make sure that you are, too. Using words like "please" and "thank-you" with students and staff members encourages students to do the same. You can stress taking turns by encouraging them to go first sometimes. Also, consider your voice: tone, volume, and word choice. Sometimes the best way to get students' attention when things get noisy is to talk more softly. Often, they will quiet down to hear what you are saying. Yelling doesn't get you far. After you have used this tactic, they might think that yelling is considered acceptable in the classroom.

Also, be an advocate for students with other staff members. When you talk to other staff members, be sure that you are talking in a positive way. If you are talking about how to handle a difficult situation with a student, discuss progress and the problems in a way that conveys that you are looking for a solution. If you hear another frustrated teacher talking about a student that she is having trouble with, be willing to suggest and share strategies that have been effective. Be quick to point out the strengths that the child possesses and ways to build on them.

Keep in mind that sometimes the teachers who teach elective classes are not aware of family circumstances that may be having an adverse effect on behavior or progress. Help them by providing information in a professional way and sharing with them some strategies that you use so that they, too, can encourage the cooperative efforts in the classroom. Often, when teachers are especially stressed about a student that they are having difficulty with, it is easier to say inappropriate things. It is important that we do not spread negativity to other teachers.

Student Talk

A good way to earn students' respect is to treat them with respect. Talk to students in a way that you would want them to talk to you. Speaking to children with sarcasm is not the way to encourage children to speak appropriately or to build their self-confidence.

Don't talk about a student or her behavior with another adult in front of the student without including her in the conversation. Venting in this manner is counterproductive and can be hurtful.

Keep your cool. If you feel that you are at the end of your rope with a student, it is not good to continue to engage in conversation. Arrange a time-out by sending him to a work station or the office or arranging for him to spend time with another teacher for a short time.

Don't put a student in a situation where she is made to feel defensive. She is likely to come out fighting, and everyone loses. Provide her choices that you both can live with.

Watch out for absolute statements, such as "You never have your homework." These can turn into self-fulfilling prophesies.

Change is a process, so don't expect overnight success. Encourage and recognize progress. Be consistent with consequences.

Teacher Talk

Spreading negativity to teachers is not modeling good behavior. A way to avoid this is by not participating in conversations that talk negatively about students' abilities, their family situations, or perceived weaknesses. Making fun of a child is never funny or acceptable. Ask yourself how you would feel if this discussion were about your child or relative. Remember that being silent when these conversations are taking place implies agreement. You need to speak up in a non-confrontational way and say something positive or in some way clarify your position. Before you leave the situation you could make a comment such as:

"Kara could be trying. I wonder how well I would do in her circumstances."

"Isn't it amazing how Travis manages to stay so cheerful and positive when learning is so hard for him".

"I look forward to seeing Nicole's smile each morning."

"Don't you just love the way Larry sees the world."

Positive Personals: Encouraging Good Behavior

Personalized Postcards

Once you have seen that your efforts to teach children to work together are showing more each day, it is important to put each student in the spotlight and acknowledge their individual strengths and new skills. As you get to know students and encourage them to be contributing members of the classroom community, it is important to remember that all students have something to offer. Many behavior problems stem from a child's lack of self-esteem or poor self-image. A postcard sent in the mail or a note with a positive message slipped into a child's cubby can make a difference. Documenting the positive behaviors is a great way to see the progress that students are making, helps you to keep parents informed of the good things that their children are doing, and encourages you to continue the positive habits you are developing in students! It is equally important to recognize the good; the bad is often easier to remember (even without documentation). Focus on the improvements that you see!

Personalized Postcards

Everyone loves to get mail—especially children. With personalized postcards, you can recognize small improvements students may make in daily interactions with others, as well as communicate those efforts to parents. Too often, the only personal correspondence some parents get from the school contains bad news. Postcards are a quick, easy way to praise students for positive behavior and help build self-esteem. This is especially effective for students who have a difficult time getting messages home. Postcards are easy to make and inexpensive to mail. Create four postcards on bright, colorful cardstock and cut them out (see page 73). Write a brief note on the back of the postcard to either the student or the parent. Both the parent and the student will be proud of the good behavior, and parents will be thrilled to receive a positive contact from you.

Dear Mr. Michaels,

I know you must be really proud of your son! Today he worked so well with his math group. I know you are working at home to help him, too. Keep up the good work!

Mrs. Smith

Clayton Michaels
555 Jones Road
Green, CA 12345

GREAT NEWS FROM SCHOOL!

Dear Margaret,

You showed real courage today when you apologized to Carter.

Keep up the positive efforts!

Mrs. Smith

Margaret Evans
808 Brown Road
Green, CA 12345

Nice Notes

Everyone can use a little reminder of encouragement for a job well done! Copy these notes on colored cardstock, cut them apart, and leave them on your students' desks to let them know you care and to brighten their day! You can personalize them by writing a specific note on the back.

Thank you for being my helper!	You really made my day!
I'm so glad you're part of our class!	Today was a rough day, but tomorrow will be better!
You had a super day!	I'm so proud of you!
What an improvement!	Way to go!
You really made a difference today!	Keep up the good work!

Fishing for Friendly Behavior

One way to reward and encourage good behavior is to keep a supply of cutout fish. Attach a strip of hook-and-loop tape to the back. When you witness positive actions, such as a student remembering to say thank you, or going out of his way to help a peer, place a fish on his desk. He then puts his name on the fish and returns it to a fish bowl. Hold a weekly or monthly fishing trip with the fish collected. You may need to start with a daily fishing trip to entice the students to perform positive actions. Then, taper off to just once a week or month. Make a simple fishing pole from a piece of bamboo or a thick stick. Attach a piece of string to one end of the pole. On the end of the string attach a piece of hook-and-loop tape (the complementary side from the tape on the fish). Select a student to go fishing for a name, and the student's name that is fished out from the bowl receives a special treat! See page 76 for a Terrific Treat List. Display the fish that have been pulled from the bowl in a special, prominent place (the wall outside the classroom door or make a bright bulletin board inside the classroom), so everyone can see the children getting caught being good. Later, you may wish to decrease the number of fishing trips to encourage more intrinsic motivation. To keep up the good behavior, offer plenty of verbal praise, notes, and other simple forms of acknowledgment.

Rewarding Record Keeping

Recognizing all of this positive behavior might get to be hard to keep track of. Did I compliment Seth this week? Have I already sent Kyra a postcard? Here are three ways to recognize individual achievement and make sure you applaud everyone's efforts equitably and timely.

• Use a seasonal notepad for each semester or month. Write one child's name on each sheet. Keep the notepad handy and each day write a kind note to one or two children listed in order in the notepad. Thank them for being helpers, turning in homework, scoring good grades, or just for being part of the class. Keep it short and encouraging!

• Print out two sets of address labels for the class. Use these when you send a Personalized Postcard home. You'll know whom you sent a card to when the student's address label is missing. You can also write the date in place of the missing label. Send at least one postcard to every child each grading period.

• Keep a Reward Record checklist of the ways and times you give positive feedback. Record each child's name on the side and indicate when you sent the child a postcard, called home, left a note on her desk, etc. (see page 77).

Terrific Treat List

1. pencil
2. folder
3. pen
4. crayons
5. colored pencils
6. eraser
7. notepad
8. homework pass
9. book
10. small toy
11. stuffed animal
12. line leader for the day
13. lunch with teacher
14. fast food gift certificate
15. kite
16. sunglasses
17. plastic jewelry
18. key chain
19. kind note
20. paper hat/crown
21. +10 on an assignment
22. school store certificate
23. poster
24. bumper sticker
25. pin/button

26. magnifying glass
27. magnet
28. gum
29. raisins
30. candy
31. choose own seat
32. extra recess time
33. candy
34. sundae
35. ice pop or ice cream
36. bookmark
37. read to a younger class
38. help in another classroom
39. extra time with favorite elective
40. greeting card
41. extra trip to library
42. extra time at favorite center
43. classroom messenger
44. choice of week's job assignment
45. sticker
46. hug or high-five
47. rubber ball
48. free-time pass
49. free class token
50. stamp

Salt Water TAFFY

Reward Record

Class List	Personalized Postcard	Nice Note	Good phone call	Special treat in locker/cubby	Positive photo on display	Work sample on display	Positive comment on work	Sticker	Other:	Other:
1										
2										
3										
4										
5										
6										
7										
8										
9										
10										
11										
12										
13										
14										
15										
16										
17										
18										
19										
20										
21										
22										
23										
24										
25										
26										
27										

Making Memorable Movies

It's All in the Presentation

Encourage students and show off the great things going on in the classroom with a video. Videos provide a fun opportunity to bring parents into school! Make a simple invitation to give to parents (see page 80). On the scheduled video premiere night, make popcorn, toss pillows on the classroom floor, and share what students are doing.

Me? Make a Video?

While you can be the director of classroom video, there is no doubt who the stars will be! It can be as simple as a short skit about sharing, you could tape parts of a typical day in the classroom, or it could be a taping of students explaining the various things that they learned in class that month. Videos can be used as a powerful tool to showcase children and what their school day looks like. After you shoot each video, invite parents in for a special showing or send the video home with each student with an explanation letter attached (see page 79).

While many would agree that videos can be a great way to communicate what is happening

Using class videos:

1. Provides a window that allows parents to see their children interacting with other students in a learning environment they might not otherwise see.

2. Allows parents to appreciate and understand the process of the learning activities, as well as the social interactions of their children.

3. Provides opportunities for parents and students to reflect on learning together, so that they can discuss classroom topics at home.

4. Provides opportunities to include parents in classroom activities so that they feel more a part of their child's success and education.

in the classroom to parents, some teachers might be intimidated with the thought of taping their class. Just remember that parents will be excited to see their children, and they won't look to see if the picture is centered or if the video is shaky. They are interested in seeing their kids at work. Since some parents don't come into the school as often as you would like, the video can show them what wonderful activities their children are doing, as well as provide an active snapshot of their child's school days. This is a great tool to build student's confidence and provide each parent some quiet time at home to observe "what Mary learned in school today." When you send a video home with the explanation letter, it's also a good idea to include a feedback ticket (see page 79). This way, you know that parents watched the video, and it gives them a chance to take an active part in the video process.

Dear Parents and Guardians,

Our class has been practicing our multiplication tables in class. We have practiced them using several different strategies, including songs, chants, and daily warm-ups. It has been so exciting to watch the students enjoy the variety of ways we have tried to learn these math facts. Enclosed is a video (showing three different math classes) and a feedback ticket. I know the students are very proud of the efforts they have made to learn their times tables, and I am certain that you will be, too! When you are finished, please return the videotape and the filled-out feedback ticket so we can share the video with another family. Thank you for your continued support!

Sincerely,
Mrs. Hughes

CRITIC'S CORNER

Well, what did you think? This is your chance to review the video. On the feedback ticket below please write your comments. Please keep it constructive. We'll be collecting feedback tickets from all parents and guardians to see how we did. Return this ticket with the video.

SHOWING.
at 6:30 p.m.
in Mrs. Jackson's classroom.
"All About Friends"
Starring Mrs. Jackson's Class
See how working together helps us to learn more!
Popcorn and pillows provided!

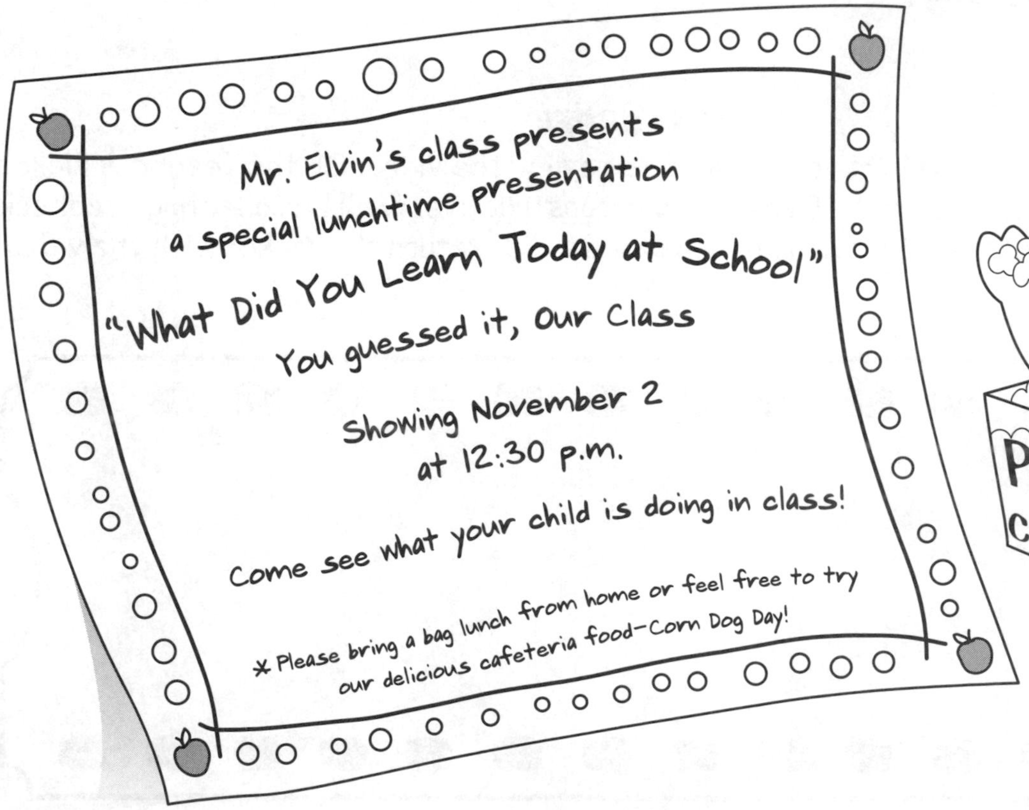
Mr. Elvin's class presents
a special lunchtime presentation
"What Did You Learn Today at School"
You guessed it, Our Class
Showing November 2
at 12:30 p.m.
Come see what your child is doing in class!
* Please bring a bag lunch from home or feel free to try
our delicious cafeteria food—Corn Dog Day!

POP
CORN

Students' Snapshots

Capture positive events to encourage more good behavior in the classroom through photography. Throughout the year, take pictures of special events like class parties or field trips and everyday events as well. Keep a disposable camera handy for student performances, small group work, or playtime activities. Display the pictures throughout the room in frames or on a designated bulletin board. Photos can capture the positive interactions between you and your students. Share the smiles you capture on film with parents by mailing a photo of their child home to them with a note. Parents will be delighted to receive a candid photo of their child at school.

Young Photographers

If you keep a digital or disposable camera handy for students, they, too, can capture you and your students working together! This will provide a great lesson in responsibility. When you assign classroom jobs each day or week, one student can be designated as the class photographer. You will need to provide some basic instruction on how to use a camera, what types of pictures to take, as well as the picture-taking limit. Once trained, he can be responsible for being on the lookout to catch his classmates exhibiting good behavior. This job assignment will help to accomplish many positive results: focusing on the positive, recognizing what good behaviors are, encouraging more daily examples of working together, and building the class photographer's confidence for handling such a big responsibility.

CAUGHT YOU CARING

Sara, Cheyene, and Reece making their project.

Ryan and Dale working with Ms. Carpas.

Tyler and Benjamin sharing their textbook.

Larry and Li hanging out on Li's first day.

Joni helping Abby and Gray with their homework.

Porsha showing Misty how to use the new software.

Imperfect Incidents:
Dealing with Difficult Situations

Understanding Anger

Diffusing Frustration

Sometimes just a change of scenery gives a child the needed opportunity to cool off and avoid an angry outburst. Often diffusing frustration before it builds further requires giving the upset student a chance to walk away and take a break physically and emotionally.

We can give students that necessary time-out by allowing them five minutes to do something that will calm them down. If children feel like they are reaching their boiling point, provide them the freedom to choose a stress reliever like modeling clay, crayons, or a small toy. For the child that enjoys music, headphones with a selection of relaxing music could be a simple break that will enable the child to cool off.

Sometimes all it takes to refocus is a positive distraction. Relaxing with deep breaths and counting to ten both often work. Another strategy includes giving the child the opportunity to run an errand outside the classroom or to organize materials in a center. Be sure that this cool-off period involves an agreed-upon safe place either in the classroom or in another supervised room. Students should never be sent to the hall or outside unattended.

Anger Sources

Children get angry for a variety of reasons. It is a natural emotion. If they can identify the source of their anger, they are more likely to develop strategies that will enable them to address it in appropriate ways. By teaching children that they often have choices in situations, we can empower them to manage their own anger and diffuse it. For example, if Suzanne knows that she often gets angry with classmates over toys at recess, she can learn how to make different toy choices to avoid those angry feelings. Likewise, if Erik learns that he gets angry when he feels rejected or ignored, then he can learn how to seek out peers that he feels comfortable joining. It is important that children be able to identify the source of anger so they can make appropriate choices to avoid difficult situations when possible. You can help discourage aggressive behavior by creating an environment in which known provocations are removed. Some problems can be prevented by anticipating difficult situations.

There are many books about anger that can help children understand that everyone gets angry and that people express their anger in different ways. This type of literature is perfect for many of the strategies and activities mentioned in this book. The Listening Center (page 22), the Reading Center (page 25), and the Caring Circle (page 34), are all opportunities in which you can incorporate these books about anger.

Advise parents of the many titles available about dealing with anger. You could make these types of books available for parents to check out, provide them a written list of books dealing with this topic, or use the books in the Backpack Connections activity (page 67), so that they can reinforce the positive efforts you are teaching at school.

Some helpful children's books that deal with anger include:

I Was So Mad
by Norma Simon and Dora Leder (Albert Whitman & Co., 1991)
This book uses simple illustrations and descriptions of situations that make children angry.

I'm Furious
by Elizabeth Crary (Parenting Press, 1996)
This is an interactive book that lets the reader choose possible reactions in situations that make people angry. Ultimately, all of the choices lead to a non-confrontational solution.

Don't Pop Your Cork on Mondays: The Children's Anti-Stress Book
by Adolph J. Moser (Landmark Editions, 1988)
Moser explores both causes and effects of stress in this book. He also offers some practical strategies for coping with stress and keeping your cool.

Don't Rant and Rave on Wednesdays: The Children's Anger-Control Book
by Adolph J. Moser (Landmark Editions, 1994)
This is a great book to use to discuss common yet inappropriate angry responses. It also offers a variety of healthy ways to control and express anger.

Anger Management Activities

Displaying Anger Solutions

When anger issues arise in class, take advantage of the opportunity to discuss the issue. The instructional time that may seem lost at the moment will be recovered later when you teach students how to react appropriately because students will be better-equipped to effectively deal with unpleasant situations when they arise. Keep a tablet of large chart paper or an erasable board to identify problem situations that include lists of possible solutions or appropriate responses. Children will enjoy the opportunity to add to the list, and it will help create an atmosphere in which everyone has quick access to find solutions to problems.

I was angry when . . .
John and Kevin laughed at my shirt.

I responded to my anger by . . .
Calling John stupid and throwing a crayon at Kevin.

I could have . . .
walked away and talked to them about it later.

What Makes Me Mad

Remind students that everyone feels angry sometimes. Stress the importance of learning how to express feelings of anger in appropriate ways. Give students a chance to tell the class about things or situations that make them angry. List their responses on the board or on chart paper. At the end of the discussion have students help you group the items listed into sets with common themes such as hurt feelings, feeling left out, having possessions misused, or being treated unfairly. Choose a situation that many children shared. Discuss what happened to cause the anger, how students handled the shared anger experience, and what the most effective strategies were. Give students a chance to offer alternative solutions or a strategy that may have worked better.

As a follow-up activity, have students fold a paper in thirds. Have them label the sections: I was angry when . . ., I responded to my anger by . . ., I could have . . . Then, invite students to think quietly about the last time they felt very angry and have them complete the labeled sections. When students have finished, have them share and discuss their responses. These papers can be kept in each child's portfolio for conferences or for later reflection and follow-up activities.

Jot It in a Journal

Encourage children to identify their feelings of anger and express those feelings in writing. Teach students the difference between "mad" and "annoyed." Give them opportunities to accurately describe how they are feeling by discussing some negative feelings that they might experience. Create a list of words that you generate and make it available for students. Stress the importance of identifying why they feel that way.

Today, I feel . . .

ANNOYED
MAD
UPSET
ANGRY
FRUSTRATED
IRRITATED
HURT
THREATENED
LEFT OUT

I feel this way because . . .

For example, "Today, I feel frustrated because I had a hard time understanding the math lesson," or "Today I feel hurt because Leann wouldn't sit with me at lunch." This will provide students a starting point to express their negative feelings. If students can accurately identify the emotions they are dealing with, as well as the source of their anger, they are less likely to overreact and more likely to act appropriately. Have students bring in a spiral notebook, or you can make journals out of small, three-ring binders with notebook paper added. Students should be reminded that they have a special place to go to write down their feelings when they (or you) see the need. You can also set up an area in the classroom where students have the freedom to write specifically about anger or negative feelings. Create a comfortable, private place where students can separate themselves from the group if they need to. If you have room, add a comfortable chair and a few pillows. You'll want this to be a place where students are encouraged to be honest and open about their feelings. Make pencils and notepads available to provide journals. You might find that students want to write their feelings down but are apprehensive about your reaction to what they wrote. It's important that students feel comfortable expressing those thoughts without fear that they'll be judged or reprimanded.

For younger students, or those with limited writing ability, encourage them to draw pictures to illustrate their frustration and draw possible solutions in their journals. All students should feel comfortable expressing their thoughts in their journals. Make it clear that this is not the kind of journal that will be graded. Do not mark spelling and punctuation in these notebooks. Explain to students that these are "thinking" journals, a place to write and draw to help them better understand themselves and their feelings.

Serious Situations

As hard as you try to create the best learning environment for your students, you won't always have a classroom full of kind, studious, helpful, organized, and eager learners. Sometimes you will encounter students who are disorganized, angry, and apathetic. Instead of becoming angry and resentful, it is best to be prepared for them. Develop strategies to help each child work on skills so that every child can experience success. If you concentrate on strengths instead of perceived weaknesses, you make success more achievable. On pages 86-93, there are serious classroom situations, some of which you may have already encountered. Following each situation are suggestions to prevent the situations and possible resolutions.

Unpredictable Behavior

Glenn is occasionally in a good mood, gets along with his peers, and follows directions nicely. What is troubling though, are Glenn's other moods. He sometimes goads his classmates and teacher into arguments. He often defies simple instructions. When asked to sit cross-legged style, he sits on his knees. When told to line up, he takes his time until he is told to line up immediately. These behaviors can wear even the most patient teacher's nerves. Glenn has also exhibited a few extreme behaviors. He has shouted back when gently reproached. He has even kicked a chair and thrown his pencil down. Nothing is ever his fault, and he often yells. His school records indicate that his home life is very dysfunctional. While Glenn truly does have plenty to be angry about, he obviously needs to learn some coping skills.

What can you do to help a child in this situation?

Confer with the school counselor.

Keep accurate, dated documentation.

Give choices when possible.

Don't emotionally back him in a corner.

Remain calm. Count to ten, if needed.

Don't let him goad you into arguing.

Reprimand gently and in private.

Don't humiliate him.

Install a time-out signal, one that you or he can use when his anger "gets to 10."

Provide him with a "Today I feel" journal response sheet.

Get to know him so you can discover his interests and use them in conversation.

Let him know you care.

Focus on strengths.

Reward small steps.

What strategies can you implement to help a child in this situation?

Focus on good qualities of the student.

Give one assignment at a time for her to work on.

Set a quiet timer to keep her on task for small time periods.

When assignment A is finished, give assignment B.

Have an extra set of textbooks available—a set at home for homework/study and a set at school.

Have her maintain a simple assignment notebook and folder—graded papers go in one pocket and homework papers to be completed and returned go in another pocket.

Check to see if she wrote down the assignments at the end of each day in the notebook.

Dealing with Disorganization

Brittany is a very intelligent student. She can solve challenging problems and is reading above grade level, but the gradebook shows several failing grades. Brittany rarely turns in homework, and she needs several reminders to return in-class assignments. They seem to quickly disappear into her desk and are hard to recover. The few papers she turns in are crumpled and messy. Her desk and folders are constantly in disarray. She is rarely on task during lessons. During a conference, Brittany's parents lament that her room is a mess, and she doesn't pay attention. It is clear that Brittany is disorganized. She has the academic ability but desperately needs organizational skills.

Keep a designated basket, bin, or folder for students to place completed papers.

Assign a student study buddy to check that assignments are copied in her notebook and papers are turned in the bin.

Keep consistent communication with parents about progress.

Maintain a homework contract with her and parents.

At the end of the school day, have all students conduct a quick book bag check.

Recognize successes.

Helping with Shyness

Marty is a good student and is usually very quiet. She often shies away from group activities and keeps to herself much of the time. When the class lines up for lunch or specials, Marty hangs back and often walks several feet behind the class. She is always the last to join a reading group or come to the carpet for group activities. It could be that Marty is shy and prefers to be by herself. On the other hand, it could be that Marty does not feel like part of the group and needs help joining. This pattern of keeping to herself may worsen as she gets older. Besides, waiting for her to catch up all the time takes up valuable instructional time and draws negative attention to Marty.

What can you do to help a child in this situation?

Talk to the student and ask her how she feels about being in your class. Does she see any problems?

Conference with parents to see if this behavior is exhibited at home.

Offer her suggestions to encourage more comfortable social interactions.

Talk to the school counselor about including her in a friendship group.

Make her line leader or give her another job assignment or classroom responsibility.

Assign her a spot in the line next to a student that she feels comfortable .

Assign a job in the reading circle, such as passing out books, so she needs to be ready with the group.

Let her know that you are there for her when needed.

Assign her to partners or groups that include students who will reach out and include her in activities.

Reward her for efforts.

Encourage staff members to give encouragement to her or notice the special things about her.

Inappropriate Talk

Tommy is usually a delightful child who learns quickly. He has many older friends and a great wit. However, when talking to adults, Tommy sometimes tries to talk like he is an adult, often using questionable language. He can find himself in trouble and often is unsure how he got there. What strategies can you implement to help a child in this situation?

When this behavior happens, speak to him privately about the specific incident.

Agree on a code word or signal that you will use to warn the student when the behavior appears to be starting.

Ask him to write a note explaining what was said, what he meant, and what would have been appropriate to say.

Discuss what kind of language and conversation topics are appropriate for students.

Help him learn ways to handle situations that have gone awry by apologizing and restating what was said.

Talk to his parents about ways they can reinforce your efforts at home.

If the behavior persists, administer a consequence and inform the parents.

Belligerent Behavior

Chris deals with his anger by striking out at others. He does not appear to acknowledge responsibility for his actions and must have the last word. Whenever he is corrected, he has a comeback which is often inappropriate. What can you do to help a child in this situation?

Talk to the student in private. Discuss the behavior that began the exchange and the consequences for that action.

Talk to the student's parents about the behavior and work together to correct it at home and at school.

Refer him to the school counselor so he can be included in a group for anger management or counseling.

Follow through on your promise to provide a consequence if he continues to argue or make remarks.

Be aware that the student might intentionally test your patience. Be prepared and stay calm.

Let your principal know what your plan is so that she can support you.

Troublesome Tardiness

Kimmy is late for school several times each week. She is never very late but consistently comes three to five minutes after the bell rings. This disrupts your morning routine and causes Kimmy to begin the day in catch-up mode. She doesn't have time to organize materials, order lunch, or visit with friends. The class is beginning to resent the time they have to wait for her to get caught up with where they are. What strategies can you implement to help a child in this situation?

Note:
It is important to be mindful of special circumstances and issues that students and their families might be experiencing. Sometimes what we might observe as a major inconvenience to our classroom could be a much more serious problem, such as school avoidance or other major issues. That is why it so crucial to maintain contact with your school's guidance department and to develop relationships with students and parents, if possible.

Talk with the student in private about what causes her to be late.

Discuss the problem with her parents, explain the problems that beginning the day late is causing. Consider the idea that they might be unaware of the problem. Home clocks could be set behind school time or they might not be aware of the school schedule.
Offer them suggestions:

Brainstorm ideas with the parents to make mornings go smoother such as preparing lunches, packing book bags, and laying out clothes the night before.

If waking up is a problem, maybe bedtime needs to be moved up so that the child gets enough sleep.

No TV in the morning can help keep everyone focused on getting ready for school.

Suggest that the child take the bus to avoid the problem.

Keep the school counselor or social worker informed of your concerns. There may be policies in place that will encourage compliance.

Unhealthy Competition

Steve, Jimmy, and Marcus often play together and usually get along well. Lately, John has been trying to join the group, and this sometimes causes problems. John and Marcus have very strong personalities and are very competitive. Lately, there have been problems at recess time with arguing and name-calling. Today, tempers flared again, and John and Marcus exchanged punches. Their stories do not match, emotions are running high, and everyone is talking at once.

What can you do to help the children in this situation?

Separate the disagreeing students to give them a chance to cool off.

Have each of them write you a letter about what happened. Who was involved? How did the problem get started? Did you see what happened or just hear about it? Who witnessed the incident? Tell exactly what happened. Have each student include a signature. After you have collected the letters, have each child come to you individually and read the letter to you. Ask questions about anything that is unclear or that you need more information about.

Call all parties together after these conversations and come to an agreement about what happened. Undoubtedly there will be discrepancies in the stories. Further discussion will clear these up.

Talk about the real issues and how they could have come to better solutions than fighting. Should they separate from each other for awhile? Is it best at times to walk away? Does it matter who hits first? Is hitting back a solution? Who could they tell to get help in solving their problems?

Decide on appropriate consequences for the event. Also, discuss what the consequences will be if this happens again.

Notify the parents and the principal.

Fragile Friendship

Lavinia, Ginnie, and Crystal have been friends for a long time. Suddenly, Ginnie has taken a leadership role in the group and has been pitting Lavinia and Crystal against each other. She chooses to play with one girl at a time, leaving the other feeling left out. Both girls are uncomfortable and unhappy but are unsure about what to do. Parents have been calling saying that their daughters are upset, complain about stomachaches, and their child does not want to come to school.

What strategies can you implement to help the children in this situation?

Talk to the girls separately to hear their sides of the story.

Bring them together and talk through their problems.

See if the counselor can work with them on friendship skills.

Encourage them to expand the number of people in their group by making other friends.

Explain how sometimes even best friends need space in their relationships, and time away can make the friendship stronger.

Try new seating arrangements.

When working in small groups, give each girl a chance to work with other classmates.

Lack of Direction and Support

Ralph is an average student who generally pays attention during class; however, he does not complete homework assignments. Ralph doesn't seem to mind making up the missed work at recess, but he is getting behind because he has so many late papers to make up. Notes home and phone calls have proven fruitless. It also takes many reminders for permission slips and field trip money to come back. Ralph seems on his own where schoolwork is concerned. Although Ralph certainly needs to develop responsibility, it seems unfair to continually punish him for home factors that are out of his control.

Note: Some of the strategies recommended may seem like extraordinary accommodations, but consider your goal. If you want to provide positive reinforcement and develop responsibility, that can happen with these modifications. Ralph and his fellow classmates are also developing even more important tools essential for continued success—self-confidence and responsibility.

What can you do to help the child in this situation?

Communicate with the parents in a conference or phone call to outline strategies. Even if they cannot offer much help, you can determine if they will participate in some way. Be realistic; you and the child might have to solve the problem yourselves.

Write reminder notes to students and attach them to work folders or notebooks.

Develop a contract with the student that includes a positive reward.

Modify the amount of homework.

Allow him more time in class to work on assignments.

Limit the days that homework is given.

Post the week's homework each Monday. Have students copy the schedule.

Coordinate test and homework schedules with other teachers.

Provide incentives for on-time assignments.

Display a classroom incentive chart so all students are working on this area.

Establish a recess club for students to stay in from recess to work on make-up assignments.

Don't expect perfection.

Focus on strengths.

Some suggestions for parents that can help their children understand and manage angry feelings in a healthy way include:

Model responsible behavior. Children pay close attention to how adults around them act in certain situations. It is important for us to model responsible anger management and express anger in non-aggressive ways.

Catch the child being good. Reinforce positive behavior. This doesn't mean that the child always needs to receive a candy treat or tangible reward. The act of acknowledgment sends a strong message as well. ("I love the way you picked up your room without being told." "Thank you for being so helpful with your sister." "I'm proud of you for being so kind to the neighbor.")

Provide opportunities for the child to discuss his feelings with you in a calm, relaxed manner.

Parents as Partners

As we teach children to become their best, we often find ourselves educating the parents as well. Children often emulate the kind of behavior they see at home. It can be helpful to explain to parents the kinds of strategies you are using in the classroom and the rationale behind them. Some parents may be aware their child has a problem expressing anger, but lack the parenting skills to assist the child in developing strategies to correct it. And while they may want to be supportive, they may not know how. When possible, include parents in the plan to help them help their children.

Express interest in the child's feelings. Validate her feelings by listening closely when she shares her thoughts. Sometimes children want to be heard, and those who feel as though no one listens are more likely to be aggressive.

Set children up for success. Avoid placing children in situations that will provoke anger. Give children opportunities to make choices to avoid negative situations.

Ignore inappropriate behavior. If the behavior is not harmful to people or property, ignore the child's behavior. Be calm and nonresponsive to the behavior, but be careful that you don't ignore the child.

Show affection. Demonstrate your love for your child and show them affection. Sometimes a hug or a physical interaction can help the child find control and comfort.

Time-Out for Teachers

As you strive to share anger management strategies with students, you will probably have moments when you need to count to ten. You will face difficult situations with difficult students. Remember that you are the model for behavior. Regardless of what is taught, children pay attention to what is practiced. Children also pay attention to verbal and nonverbal messages. If they feel that you care about them, they are more likely to be receptive to discipline, correction, or suggestions. The following tips offer practical, common sense reminders for moments when you must keep your cool and maintain a positive example.

Maintain your sense of professionalism. NEVER engage in name-calling or threats. Remember that as you interact with a student who is being difficult, he is watching how you control yourself, as are other students present.

Even when you are frustrated with a student, be careful to maintain a sense of confidentiality when discussing students with colleagues, and always hold these conversations in a private setting rather than the lounge or hallway where others could overhear.

Don't discuss a student's behavior with another teacher in front of the student. Unless you have asked another teacher to join you to conference with the child, talking about specific students with other teachers in front of children will not build trusting relationships.

Remain as calm as you can. Some students will test you, and some may try to engage in a verbal confrontation with you. When they do, make sure that they realize that they are contributing members of the classroom community, but they will not control the class. Be sure they understand that while you may not like what they did, you do like them.

Don't allow situations to escalate into chaos. Teachers don't have to micromanage every interaction to maintain structure in the classroom. If you see students interacting in a way that could lead to a conflict, provide options that will enable students to diffuse the situation.

Give students choices and provide them with ownership over their decisions as well as clearly defined consequences. If they feel they have no control, many students will feel the effort isn't worth it.

Make all students feel welcome every day. Greet each student by name at the beginning of each day and smile, especially to students who may have been disruptive the day before. Students need to feel that each day is a new day.

Offering Extra

Some students need a little extra—whether they are categorized with special needs or not. Whatever the need may be, modifying assignments may be necessary. Success is the goal, and some children need help to experience it. These modifications require little extra preparation except a thorough knowledge of your students and the desire to want to see them work together more effectively in the classroom.

High achievers need extra, too!
Give more challenging spelling words.

Encourage them to go above and beyond your expectations on projects.

Provide higher-level assignments.

Put together work packets to keep them moving forward.

Provide the opportunity for choices.

Allow them to work together on a more challenging assignment.

For students overwhelmed by work, visually reduce the amount of work in front of the child by crossing out a few problems or cutting off the bottom portion of a worksheet.

Give a poor speller an abbreviated spelling list. When she has experienced success with fewer words, gradually add a few more to the list until she is up to the regular amount.

Allow a disorganized child to sit at a larger table. He likely needs more space to spread out and feel comfortable. Also, keep an extra set of textbooks in the classroom.

Allow a fidgety child to take breaks, such as sharpening pencils, checking the mail, or passing out materials (as long as this is not used as an opportunity to cause commotion in class).

For students struggling with handwriting, allow them to type assignments occasionally. For those that struggle with reading, conduct an assignment or test aloud. This allows the child to focus on the material being learned rather than straining to write or read it.

For a student experiencing angst over a test question, offer a hint or take one possible answer away on a multiple choice test.

If there is little support at home to help with homework, set up a study group at recess or in the morning to prevent children from receiving a week's worth of failed homework.

Make audiotape textbooks available to students. If these aren't supplied by your textbook company, have volunteers read and record the material.